MAXIMUM CONTROL

MASTERING YOUR HEAVYWEIGHT BIKE

PAT HAHN

WITH STEVE GUDERIAN AND
MARK BROWN

PHOTOGRAPHY BY
DARRYL AND LORI CANNON

motorbooks

First published in 2009 by Motorbooks, an imprint of MBI Publishing Company, 400 First Avenue North, Suite 300, Minneapolis, MN, 55401 USA

MBI Publishing Company titles are also available at discounts in bulk quantity for industrial or sales-promotional use. For details write to Special Sales Manager at MBI Publishing Company, 400 First Avenue North, Suite 300, Minneapolis, MN, 55401 USA

To find out more about our books, visit us online at www.motorbooks.com.

Library of Congress Cataloging-in-Publication Data

Hahn, Pat, 1969-
  Maximum control : mastering your heavyweight bike / Pat Hahn.
    p. cm.
  ISBN-13: 978-0-7603-3674-8 (pbk. : alk. paper)
  ISBN-10: (invalid) 0-7603-3674-2 (pbk. : alk. paper)
 1. Motorcycling. 2. Motorcycling–Safety measures. 3. Motorcycling accidents--Prevention. 4. Motorcycles. I. Title.

  TL440.5.H355 2010
  629.28'475–dc22
                        2009022787

On the cover: Photo by Kevin Wing

On the frontis: One of the most popular heavyweight motorcycles ever built: Harley-Davidson's Electra Glide.

On the title page: American Honda Motor Co.

About the author
Pat Hahn can answer just about any question related to motorcycle safety, be it knowledge, skills, technical, or theoretical. He is especially familiar with the concepts of risk management, hazard awareness, crash avoidance, and traction management as they pertain to motorcycle riders. . Pat is an MSF-Certified Instructor (12 years), author of the motorcycle skill books *How to Ride a Motorcycle* and *Ride Hard, Ride Smart*, co-author of *Motorcycle Track Day Handbook*, and Public Information Officer for the State of Minnesota, where he coordinates public information and education for the Minnesota Motorcycle Safety Center, a project of the Minnesota Department of Public Safety. He lives in Minneapolis, Minnesota.

About the photographers
Darryl and Lori Cannon are co-owners of killboy.com, a motorsports photography website centered around the world-famous section of U.S. Highway 129 known as the "Tail of the Dragon." Killboy.com employs four full-time people: Darryl, his wife Lori, and two additional photographers.

Their work has been published in dozens of magazines and featured on many commercial websites. If you have ever visited or plan to slay the Dragon in the future, be sure to look for your photos by the original Dragon photographer.

Editor: Darwin Holmstrom
Design Manager: Kou Lor
Designer: Chris Fayers
Cover designer: Simon Larkin

Printed in China

Contents

About the Authors

Pat Hahn is a motorcycle rider with over 20 years of experience and the author of *Ride Hard, Ride Smart* and *How to Ride a Motorcycle*. For 12 years he has been an MSF-certified instructor/rider coach for the state of Minnesota teaching basic and experienced rider courses. Since 1999, Pat has managed public relations for the Minnesota Motorcycle Safety Center, an award-winning program known nationwide for its informational and educational campaigns. He also works as a consultant for other states and has conducted technical assessments of motorcycle safety programs in Colorado, Ohio, Florida, and California.

With volunteer help from the Central Roadracing Association, Pat also conducts advanced cornering and safety seminars for Minnesota sportbike enthusiasts (www.hedonistic-enthusiasm.com). He is a freelance editor and writer, contributing to Evans Brasfield's *101 Sportbike Performance Projects* and Kent Larson's *Track Day Handbook*, as well as writing numerous articles for *Minnesota Motorcycle Monthly* and other enthusiast publications. Pat uses his bike (currently a Honda VFR800FI) to commute to work, run errands, entertain friends, burn off steam on twisty roads on the weekends, and take long trips. He lives with his wife and two-year-old son in south Minneapolis.

Steve Guderian is a retired motorcycle police officer, court-recognized expert in collision reconstruction, and crash investigator who now works as a government motorcycle safety expert. He is also an MSF-certified rider coach in the state of California. In the spring of 2009, Steve was one of the principal researchers in a cutting-edge research project on motorcycle rider human factors. Additionally, Steve is involved with numerous publications as a contributing writer, as well as being a member of many associations that further motorcycle safety awareness.

Steve has always had a passion for motorcycles and has ridden a wide variety of bikes, rain or shine, for more than 34 years. His greatest desire is to help educate the motorcycle community in all aspects of motorcycle safety and, more importantly, to apply that knowledge to everyday riding. Steve has a degree in physics with a minor in mathematics. He resides with his wife of 33 years in northern California, and together they have three adult daughters and three granddaughters. Steve most enjoys riding side-by-side with his wife on weekends, vacations, or whenever the opportunity arises.

Mark Brown is a North Carolina State Highway Patrolman of more than 23 years and a training coordinator within the Special Operations Motor Unit. Mark is the lead police motor instructor for all North Carolina State Highway motorcycle training and has provided training and oversight for the certification of hundreds of law enforcement motor officers in some of the most rigorous testing in the world on many types of police motorcycles. He is the president of MotoMark1 (www.motomark1.com), North Carolina's premier motorcycle training provider, and the only BikeSafe trainer in the United States.

Mark holds numerous certifications in police motor instruction, motor officer survival tactics, and combat military motorcycle training. His certifications in executive protection have afforded him the opportunities to provide presidential and vice-presidential motorcade escorts. As a marshal for numerous motor escorts, Mark has participated in events like the Kyle Petty Charity Ride across America, Olympic Torch Relay, Ultimate Drive Susan G. Koman Foundation, and Ironman Triathlon, as well as motorcycle manufacturer events. Mark lives with his wife and three children near Raleigh, North Carolina.

Acknowledgments

I am deeply grateful to Steven Guderian and Mark Brown (motomark1.com), who were my left and right hands in bringing this book together. Special thanks go to Darryl and Lori Cannon of killboy.com for their skill, hard work, and good cheer. Mad props go out to Brian Sprinkle and Robert Parrish for their wisdom and wet-weather riding skills, and to Allan Sadowski for entrusting his Gold Wing to us on slippery roads!

I also want to call out Bob Reichenberg of Streetmasters and Team Oregon fame for his keen eye and B.S. detector, and for inspiring me to finally get the Inside Line down in print. As they say, great minds think alike. Thanks to Kent Larson (*Track Day Handbook*) and Kyle Knutsen (2Kmotorsports.com) for their suspension advice. Finally, hats off to Andy Goldfine and the Rider Wearhouse (aerostich.com), who created the Aerostich suits and Darien jackets pictured throughout this book.

This book is dedicated to my uncle Pat Hahn, 1952–2009. Pat was my godfather and my guru, an enthusiast who sparked my interest at a very early age. Rest in peace, my friend. We all miss you down here.

Introduction

■ Types of Big Bikes ■ Objectives
■ How to Use this Book

Maximum control is having the attitude, knowledge, and skill that make you the master of your own two-wheeled domain. This means knowing exactly what your bike can and cannot do, knowing exactly what you as the rider can and cannot do, and perfecting the skills that allow you to make your bike do whatever you want, whenever you want.

Many riders are intimidated by big bikes. They say they're a lot to handle, that they can have a mind of their own, that one false move can send you into orbit. These things are all true. But what's also true is that a big bike is still just a machine, a tool that will do exactly what you tell it to do. You just need to know how to speak its language.

Think of mastering a big bike like taming a wild beast—breaking a horse, for example. You need to get acquainted, spend some time together, and get to know each other. You need to learn the inputs required to make it do what you want. You need to practice with it every day and learn to work as a team, build trust, and learn where the limits are—always with the understanding that you won't push it beyond these limits. Your reward after all this hard work is a trusty steed that will get you through thick and thin in all kinds of weather—on your terms.

But turning a wild beast into a trusted friend isn't something that happens in a day. Oh no. Even if it's something you've done all your life, it still takes a good amount of time, especially early on when you're just getting to know one another. And once you've cemented the friendship, it requires regular, ongoing maintenance to keep it familiar. This means frequent riding, as well as training and practicing too. Maximum control isn't something that you just develop and then have forever. It requires a commitment to be always at the top of your game. You never want to be out on a ride and find

A bike made for the solo cruising trips, with retro styling and lots of chrome. This bike was made to take you to any gathering you want to go. *American Honda Motor Co.*

The Triumph Rocket III is 2,294cc (or 2.3 liters) of engine, weighing in at over 800 pounds. The Rocket comes in bagger or cruiser styles. *Triumph Motorcycles*

Opposite: One of the most popular touring bikes is the Electra Glide. It comes with all of the basic necessities: stereo, CD player, CB radio, cruise control, and lots of storage, including soft-sided luggage specifically made for the trunk and saddlebags. Options include pretty much everything that doesn't come standard, such as satellite radio, GPS, heated seats, and handgrips. And . . . it's a Harley.

The mighty Gold Wing cockpit. There's enough there to keep you entertained all afternoon without even leaving your driveway. *American Honda Motor Co.*

> "... big bikes come in many forms–dressers/tourers, baggers, cruisers, and sport-tourers. The toughest bikes to master are 900cc on up and start at around 600 pounds."

out the hard way that you are not the one in charge.

But before we head down the road to maximum control, let's discuss big bikes.

Just What Is a Big Bike?

When we talk about big bikes, the first thing that comes to mind for most people is the touring bike, the Barcalounger on wheels. There's the big fairing up front with a built-in stereo, CD player, CB radio, drink holder, heat vents, and just about anything else you could ever want or even think of. It's got two big, hard saddlebags and an upper storage trunk, called a top case, on the back. This bike was made to take two people, of any size, anywhere they could possibly want to go, for as long they want to be gone. To do all this, a bike has to be big. And if it's big, you can bet that it's also heavy.

Is there anything bigger? You bet there is. There are two-wheel motorcycles out there with honest-to-god V-8 engines—the *Boss Hoss*, for example. They're huge. Big touring bikes generally weigh in at around 800 pounds, give or take. The *Hoss* pushes 12 bills, which makes it an awful lot of motorcycle.

But for our discussion, big bikes come in many forms—dressers/tourers, baggers, cruisers, and sport-tourers. The toughest bikes to master are 900cc on up and start at around 600 pounds. This is not to say that smaller bikes are not

tough to master or that you don't use the same techniques to ride them. They are, and you do.

What's more, motorcycle enthusiasts vary in size and weight. Some riders are what we affectionately refer to as "vertically challenged." Some weigh in at a modest 150 pounds, soaking wet. Others (you know who you are!) tip the scales daily at three-and-a-half bills and sport a seven-foot wingspan. Those 150-pound riders are going to have their work cut out for them, muscling around those 800-pound behemoths, while the 350-pound riders may have an easier time of it. The term "big bike" can take on different meanings too, depending on the rider. A 1,200 Sporty might seem like a big bike to a bantamweight novice, but it's only the starting point for those of us who are designed more like Shrek.

In the end, however, it's not as much a matter of size and strength as it is a matter of skill and practice. The rider's size and strength really only matter when the bike tries to fall over. Riding carefully (mindful of the situations in which you put yourself) and having well-developed bike-control skills can keep that from ever happening. This all boils down to the fact that riders of big bikes can most benefit from dedicated training and practice to bring the additional responsibility down to a workable level.

Think of the difference between a regular bike and a big bike like the difference between a pickup truck and a tractor-trailer combo. Both are road-going vehicles, easily piloted by one person. Both have controls like throttle, brakes, gears, and a steering mechanism. Both are relatively simple to operate once you learn the controls. But in the bigger vehicle, the operator is responsible for more size and weight, which requires more planning ahead, and the consequences of a mistake are more dramatic.

The quintessential big bike is the tried-and-true Honda Gold Wing. It's the Lexus of the big bikes. It is ready to take you anywhere in two-wheeled comfort, with XM satellite radio, tire pressure monitoring system, GPS, six-element speaker system, reverse gear, and cruise control—and it's the only bike that comes with a rider air bag.

Probably the most popular bagger in the United States today: the Harley-Davidson Street Glide. This bike was made for cruising or for a long-distance overnighter. Off the showroom floor this bike gives you a radio, a CD player, and plenty of storage. Options include everything available on the Ultra Classic dresser.

The Dresser

Also called full dressers, touring bikes, or tourers, dressers are the biggest of the big dogs, usually weighing between 700 and 900 pounds. These bikes are built to haul two people and their luggage anywhere they want to go with the comfort of stereo sound, CB radios, and just about any other electronic gadget you would want.

The Bagger

A bagger is a hybrid dresser and cruiser. These bikes range from 650 to 850 pounds. Baggers have saddlebags for storage just like the dressers, but they don't usually have rear trunks or top boxes. Treatment on the front end varies. They may have the big front fairings like the dressers, they may just have windscreens, or they may have nothing at all. Baggers can certainly carry two people, but straight off the showroom floor they're designed for just one.

The Suzuki Boulevard line has developed a good reputation and loyal following, even though it's a relative newcomer to the big-bike club. The Suzuki comes with a massive 240/40R18 rear tire, a 2-into-1-into-2 exhaust system, and two spark plugs and four valves per cylinder.

The Cruiser

A cruiser is just what its name implies: a day-tripper weighing between 600 and 800 pounds meant for cruising around all day or just cruising out to get a bite to eat. There are no bags, and there is no trunk or other storage, though often owners add leather or leather-like saddlebags. Cruisers may have windscreens or they may not. Many come with detachable windscreens. In general, these bikes are designed for a single rider, though the accessories to make a cruiser friendly for two-up riding are readily available.

The Sport-Tourer

Another hybrid motorcycle, the sport-tourer ranges in weight from the high 500s to the 700-pound range. This bike is a cross between a bagger and a sportbike. Sport-tourers are built for spirited riding and cornering like a sportbike, but they have comfortable riding positions and room for long legs, making them ideal candidates for long trips and mountain passes. The removable hard bags offer enough room to pack away a few things for overnight trips or camping, and the wind protection is generally very good.

Okay, I Get It. Big Bikes are Heavy. What are Some of the Other Differences?

Weight isn't the only thing that sets big bikes apart from the crowd. The geometry of the bikes usually includes a longer wheelbase and a lower center of gravity. This generally makes the bike more stable and confidence-inspiring to ride, but this comes at the expense of maneuverability—a bike built for stability requires more work to get it turned.

On the other hand, braking is a little easier on big bikes than other bikes. Big bikes have big, powerful brakes, and the front-to-rear braking power is more balanced. The rear brake does a lot more of the work of stopping a big bike than it does on lighter bikes, especially sportbikes. A Yamaha R1 (1,000cc) sportbike probably uses 90 to 100 percent front brake and 0 to 10 percent rear brake in a hard stop. A Harley-Davidson Road King probably uses more like 70 to 80 percent front brake and 20 to 30 percent rear brake. So stopping a big bike quickly is a little easier to learn and a lot easier to perfect. In fact, big cruisers can stop just as quickly, if not quicker, than many top-of-the-line sportbikes.

Riders get some other benefits from riding big bikes too. Having hard-mounted luggage and storage space as an integral part of the bike means you can just pick up and go whenever the mood strikes you. How's that for freedom? Once you're on the road, you're usually behind some kind of windshield or fairing. This insulates you from wind and the effects of temperature, which can delay the onset of fatigue and allow you to ride longer. And the comfortable seating position and big gas tanks mean you don't have to stop as often—big bikes can really help you make time on a long trip.

The Yamaha FJR1300 revolutionized the sport-touring bike niche. Smooth, even power, reliable handling, and cutting-edge aerodynamic bodywork make this one of the most popular sport-touring bikes. The FJR1300 comes with an adjustable front windscreen, ABS brakes, plenty of storage, and enough electrical output to run plenty of add-ons, such as auxiliary lights, heated grips and clothing, and GPS.

This is the Fat Boy, a longtime favorite of the Harley-Davidson Softail line, which is one of the longest lines of production cruisers. The Fat Boy features classic styling with modern touches, such as solid wheels; six-speed transmission; 96 inches (1,584cc) of Twin-Cam, V-Twin power; and chrome, dual-shotgun exhaust.

One of the disadvantages of riding a big bike is having to compensate for poor planning when there's a crowd of people watching you. When it comes to parking, it pays to take your time and really scope out a spot that won't cause you trouble when you return to your bike.

There are other benefits as well. Riding and enthusiast clubs pop up around the most popular bikes, so you don't have to look too far to find a group of like-minded individuals to hook up with and ride. With the advent of the Internet, advice from experts is only a few keystrokes away, whether you're trying to troubleshoot a weird engine noise, looking for tips on passing the endorsement test, or deciding what tire to choose. The popularity of big bikes also means there's a wide availability of aftermarket goodies, making it easy to customize your bike and make it truly your own.

There are a couple of drawbacks to riding a big bike, though they're relatively minor. On a big bike you give up some of the advantages that a small, svelte motorcycle has. A big bike is actually closer to a small economy car with regard to space requirements. Parking the bike on the street can sometimes be a challenge. Not only does the bike take up more room—two big dressers cover the same area as four smaller bikes—but finding just the right parking spot (and deciding which end goes in first) is important too. Parking requires planning ahead so you don't end up having to duck walk an 800-pound bike backward up a sandy incline.

Objectives

The primary objectives for maximum control of your heavyweight motorcycle are simple: 1) be smooth, 2) plan ahead, 3) keep something in reserve, and 4) practice.

At 10 years old, Victory is the new kid on the block for cruising and touring motorcycles. The Victory Vision is the company's latest and most radical touring model. Its unique styling is either love-it or hate-it (we love it). The Anniversary Edition comes with all of the standard amenities of your top-of-the-line touring bike, along with a reverse gear, XM radio, and GPS. The 10th Anniversary Edition is truly a marvelous motorcycle, and all 100 of these models sold out in seven minutes online. *Victory Motorcycles*

BIG-BIKE MYTHS

Big bikes are harder to stop than smaller bikes.
False. Even though big bikes are heavier, they're equipped with big brakes designed to handle the job. All bikes are designed so that an average person can stop the bike quickly and efficiently, with or without luggage and a passenger. We'll discuss braking in Chapters 6 and 7.

First response to any bad situation should be to brake.
False. While braking is almost always a better first choice than swerving to avoid a conflict, braking isn't necessarily the end-all response. Think about it. The power-to-weight ratio of most motorcycles means that robust acceleration is at your fingertips. Getting on the gas is often as viable an option as braking, if it can get you out of a bad spot before a situation even develops.

My wife and I have to get matching outfits.
True. Your passenger should wear all the same gear you wear. This means, at a minimum, a helmet, a jacket, boots, and gloves. Of course we're kidding; you don't have to get all matchy-matchy like some folks do . . . but doing so may help you blend in with the couples in your riding club. There will be more on riding gear in the Riding Strategy section of this chapter.

If it falls over, I won't be able to pick it up.
False. We're not saying it's *easy*, but most healthy people, of any size or stature, can lift a fallen bike if they know the technique. The trick is to use the biggest, strongest muscles in your body, rather than your back or arms or shoulders. We'll show you how to do it in Appendix A.

Big bikes take more effort to steer.
True. Big-bike geometry and mass both make the bike want to continue in a straight line rather than turn. Steering requires focused and deliberate handlebar inputs, and a little muscle tone, to get it right. Fortunately, big bikes are not all that much harder to steer than smaller bikes—it's more getting used to how much force is required to get the lean you want. We'll discuss steering and cornering in Chapters 8 and 9.

Big bikes can't be used for commuting or everyday use.
False. Sure, the higher calling of big bikes is to put on the miles, but that doesn't mean you can't use them for riding to work and back, running up to the store, and general day-to-day stuff. It's like the pickup truck versus the tractor-trailer again: sure, it's a little less work to run around in the smaller vehicle, but the bigger one is still meant to be used every day. They sag and mope and get dusty when you leave them sitting. In fact, if you ever want your riding to improve at all, you *have* to ride your big bike every day. If you ride it only once or twice a week, you'll always be rusty, and you'll always look like a beginner.

There are two kinds of riders: those who have gone down and those who will.
False. There's nothing written that says just because you ride a motorcycle, you'll crash it. I mean, everybody makes mistakes, and it's likely you'll have an unplanned get-off some day, but it ain't written in the stars. Thinking hard about your riding, practicing every time you ride, and being careful about the situations in which you put yourself are the keys to keeping the shiny side up. Motorcycle safety means skilled decision-making.

1) ***Be smooth.*** The best approach to mastering a big bike is to be smooth over everything else, as opposed to just "getting the job done." Motorcycles don't respond to jerky, imprecise inputs very well. Being smooth means you'll have to give yourself a little more room to work at first, but the reward is worth the effort. The bike will be more predictable and handle better, and you'll cut a more impressive profile out on the street.

2) ***Plan ahead.*** This means anticipating what's coming up next, knowing what to expect, and planning to be in control of whatever situation lies around the bend. From finding the perfect parking spot, to setting up for a corner, to maximum braking in an emergency, by the time you're actually executing the maneuver, your mind is already on the next maneuver. Planning ahead helps keep you from getting caught in a bad situation. If you find

Another perfectly styled bike for cruising out to your favorite dinner spot, be it an hour away or a week away. Instead of a stereo-laden fairing, the Nomad comes with an adjustable windscreen, 1,700cc motor, six-speed transmission, and plenty of storage in two hard-sided saddlebags. Another great thing about this motorcycle is that it's big enough and roomy enough to take your favorite companion to dinner with you. *Kawasaki Motors Corp.*

"Just like playing cards, don't show your hand until you have to."

yourself thinking too hard about what you're doing at the moment, or you keep getting surprised by what the road is throwing at you, you're not planning far enough ahead. Slow down and give your brain more time to work.

3) *Keep something in reserve.* Just like playing cards, don't show your hand until you have to. On a racetrack, competitors are riding at 100 percent of their ability, and when things go wrong, it usually means a crash because there's nothing left in their bag of tricks. They've let it all hang out and got bit by it. On the street, ride somewhere closer to 80 percent—you're still getting the job done, but you've got an ace or two up your sleeve if and when you need it.

4) *Practice.* The single biggest obstacle to maximum control is not getting enough time in the saddle. If you only ride once or twice a week, you'll always be more or less a beginner at the controls. To be any good at all, and to get better, requires

a commitment to using the bike as often as you can—every day, if possible. If your brain is going to have a "default" driving mode, you want it to be a two-wheeled frame of mind, not a four-wheeled frame of mind.

Mental Practice
One method of practice is visualization. Athletes understand the value of visualization and use it to enhance their performance. Strong visualization practice and purposeful mental concentration can help them get closer to perfection in their skills, moves, and reactions—before ever setting foot on the playing field. Playing an active role in their imaginations, seeking out hypothetical situations, and mentally going through the motions helps prepare them for the time when they may need to make those exact moves.

For example, while someone like Tiger Woods is standing over a difficult shot, taking practice swings,

The BMW RT is one of the longest-running sport-touring models. It is noted for exceptional performance and long-distance touring capabilities. This bike has a lot of space for storage, heated grips and seat, a premium sound system, cruise control, and standard ABS brakes. The long list of options for this motorcycle includes on-the-fly, pushbutton electronic suspension controls.

evaluating and reevaluating the layout, he's also visualizing exactly how he wants the next shot to go. He sees himself swinging at the ball with exactly the right speed and direction, he sees the ball arcing away perfectly to the height and distance he wants, he sees it drop and bounce and come to a stop in the perfect position for his next shot. Once he sees how it's all going to go, he bears down on the ball, scoops it up, and presto! It does pretty much what he expected. (That's no coincidence. Imagine if he'd been afraid of a bad swing and instead visualized the ball sculling across the ground, bonking into a tool shed, and landing in a pond. Or what if he'd instead visualized nothing at all? This can be the bad side of visualization—see and believe something bad is going to happen, therefore, you make it happen. It's another example of a common, self-fulfilling prophecy.)

The technique of visualization can also work for motorcyclists. I'm not talking about the "What If?" game that we play to identify hazards while we're actually in the riding environment. I'm talking about the power of positive thinking: dreaming up situations, examining your options, and then visualizing yourself reacting perfectly to the situation—and doing this all from the comfort of your favorite chair.

Build the whole scene in your head. See yourself in the cockpit of your bike. Your gloves, your jacket, your gas tank are all familiar. Put yourself on a familiar road. Now, see yourself approach a situation, imagine all the possible outcomes, decide on the one best outcome, and make it happen. See your hands and feet move in response, see your bike change position, speed, or direction to correct the situation, and see the hazard disappear in your rearview mirrors.

Visualization, a technique very useful in sports, is also useful to a rider looking to hone his or her mental and physical strategies and skills. When training, professional athletes work every angle to prepare their minds and practice overcoming every conceivable obstacle—before they have to do it in real time. They visualize the layout, conditions, and hazards, and they develop strategy in their heads. When the time comes to perform, they've conditioned their minds and bodies to react skillfully. When they're faced with a tough situation, they've already visualized it, solved it—practiced it.

In the real world, if you need to brake suddenly down to 15 from 60 miles per hour, then make a quick swerve to the left around an animal, then accelerate quickly away to avoid getting rear-ended, the whole thing will go over better if you've done it in your mind a few times and have a ready response.

By working through various riding situations from the safety of your imagination, you begin to develop conditioned responses to hazards that may or may not ever come your way. Being ready and familiar with even the most unusual situation gives you an edge when it comes to dealing with surprises. Being mentally well practiced conditions your body to react more in the way you want it to rather than in the way your instinct tells it to. Instinct can be a good thing, and it can also be a bad thing, especially on a motorcycle. Just imagine the natural reaction of a newer rider who enters a corner too hot and decides to focus on the guardrail! Riders need to develop the discipline to stay with it when everything else goes wrong, to have faith in their bikes and their tires, and to ride it out, rather than giving up and putting it in the weeds.

Physical Practice

Athletes understand the value of physical practice. This kind of practice builds muscle and endurance and helps your body develop the memory of the motions. Physical practice helps the motion become unconscious, instinctive, and instantaneous. It helps you achieve a good physical condition in which to participate in your sport of choice.

Your goal should be to plan to practice your skills by the day, by the week, by the month, and by the year. Every day, before you set out, decide what skill or skill component you'd like to practice during that ride. It could be balancing at slow speeds. It could be smoother braking. It could be quicker steering inputs. Decide on one thing and practice it throughout the duration of the ride. Once a week, at the end of a ride, practice a riding skill for 10 or 20 minutes before parking the bike, such as U-turns, heavy braking, clutch control, whatever. If you can show some improvement or finally get something just right when you're tired, you know that you are on your way to really building that skill.

Once or twice a month, set aside an hour or two to work on just your skills, maybe in a parking lot, maybe on a particular stretch of road you know well. Engage in a variety of exercises, working on two to four different skills, and don't quit until you feel you've shown some improvement. Then, once or twice a year, go out and find yourself

One more fine example of the cruisers that can take you one hour or one week away, any time you feel like it. *Yamaha Motor Corp.*

Being smooth, planning ahead, keeping something in reserve, and visualizing will not help you as much as all these things *plus* dedicated practice of the skills you need to perform in the real world.

some formal training. Take an annual safety course, try a track day with some professional instruction, or maybe seek out a law-enforcement agency that offers civilian training. If setting aside 15 minutes or a couple of hours is good for building skill, imagine the value of setting aside an entire day or two just to focus on you and your motorcycle, building the relationship, keeping in tune with one another. Five to ten hours of uninterrupted practice time will stick with you for at least half your riding season.

And when it comes to formal training, here are two additional

thoughts. First: train at 100 percent. You're working on building your skill set, expanding your envelope and comfort level. You can't do it, and you can't learn anything, if you're riding at 80 percent like you would on the street. Second, be sure you do your training on the bike you actually ride. No loaner bikes. No training bikes. "But I don't want to dump my bike." Tough beans. If you're going to throw that bike down, best to do it in a relatively safe, controlled environment. Pull the bags off, tape up the signals and mirrors and delicate parts or remove them, and have at it. At the end of the day, you'll be glad you did.

How to Use This Book

Maximum Control provides expert motorcycle handling information and 10 practice drills to help you develop your physical riding skills, whether you are a relative beginner or a lifelong veteran of riding. There is something for everyone in every chapter.

However, you cannot learn to ride from a book; the authors assume you have a basic level of understanding of motorcycle control and that you have taken at least a basic motorcycle-riding course, available in almost every state in the U.S. If you've never taken any motorcycle training, your first order of business is to sign up for the next available course you can find. That knowledge and practice will provide a solid base from which to practice the drills in this book. *Maximum Control* is meant to pick up where these courses leave off.

Also, the key words in the above section are *physical riding skills*. This book focuses almost solely on the *physical* aspect of riding a motorcycle and mostly ignores the mental aspects, such as riding strategy, hazard perception, positioning, and what riding gear you choose to wear. For a very brief discussion of basic riding strategy, refer to Appendix B.

The drills move from low-speed, coordinated fine-muscle-control exercises in early chapters to higher-speed, decision-making and finesse exercises in the later chapters. However, the earlier drills are not necessarily easier than the later drills. Low-speed riding is not easy. There is a risk that you'll drop your bike while practicing. Dropping your bike can result in some broken parts or some scratches you may not want to have, on your bike or yourself.

The key is to take it slow and not be in too big of a hurry to move on to the next step. Be patient with yourself—maximum control is not a skill that comes quickly. It's going to take

Rule of thumb: train at 100 percent, ride at 80 percent.

some time. We have seen new riders practicing these drills without causing any significant damage to their bikes. Oh, they dropped their bikes, all right, but because they started out slowly and only progressed forward when they were confident in themselves, the results were only a few minor scratches. But also take a moment to think about this: would you rather drop your bike when you are practicing in a safe area, or would you rather do it out in the mean streets?

Authors' Note. Throughout the book we refer to and picture using "cones" in the riding drills. This is not meant to be taken strictly literally. Cones are great, but any sort of markers work fine, such as cut-in-half tennis balls, crushed-down soda cans, or (one of the authors' favorites) full bottles of beer. (You're less likely to cut too close to the cones and knock them over, and after a hard day's practice, you can take them home, ice them down, and feast on your "enemies.")

> **"This book focuses almost solely on the *physical* aspect of riding a motorcycle . . ."**

Chapter 1

Bike Setup

▌ **Adjusting the Controls**

▌ **Tire Pressure**

▌ **Suspension Theory and Baseline Setup**

If you select the right bike, plan on growing older together. This has upsides and downsides. On the upside, you'll get to know the bike so intimately that riding it will be second nature. On the other hand, as the bike gets older and the miles pile up on the odometer, you have to work just a little harder to make it do what you want. And don't forget: you'll be getting older too. The same goes for you.

Opposite: There's nothing wrong with tweaking your bike to get it just how you like it. The authors recommend adjusting mechanical components first before you start in with the custom paint and chrome go-fasters. *Ty Huynh*

On the bike-setup spectrum, there are two opposite approaches to dealing with each bike's individual character and unique quirks. On one end are those who simply "ride around it." This means adapting your approach, your body position, and your riding style to meet the bike's demands. It can also mean not doing anything as noble as that, instead, it can mean just putting up with the bike's quirks for so long you end up getting used to them.

On the other end of the spectrum is modifying the bike. This involves adjusting or replacing various components to minimize or eliminate ergonomic, mechanical, handling, or aesthetic distractions. This route can involve a good deal of thoughtful analysis, research, time, money, and, most importantly, patience. But a rider is rewarded with a bike that is set up just for him or her, perfect in every way and ready to be used to the utmost. Of course, all the modifications in the world won't do you much good if you're not able to adapt your riding style at least a little.

The best and most popular approach is a combination of the two extremes: modify the things you can, and adapt your riding to the rest. There are quite a few things on a bike that are ready, willing, and able to be adjusted, such as the controls, suspension, and tire pressure. Other things like handlebars, brakes, and seat are easily modified but require some additional time and money as well as a little mechanical know-how. The less malleable items like ride height, wheelbase, and steering geometry are not really meant to be modified (you should have picked a different bike!), but a rider bent on making the bike absolutely perfect can still find a way if he or she is willing to spend the money.

Once you've adapted your bike to your liking, you fill in the gaps by adjusting your riding style to

"... modify the things you can, and adapt your riding to the rest."

Your reach to the bars should be 100 percent natural and comfortable. You'll want your shoulders relaxed, your arms bent at the elbows, and your hands in line with your forearms.

male. The manufacturers need to start somewhere, so they build the bike for the Average Joe. More specifically, they use market research to determine the weight, height, and preferences of the Average Joe who buys that particular model, and they tailor the bike to that person. Unfortunately, if you're instead a five-foot-four female with a 28-inch inseam, or a six-four male pushing three bills, the way the bike is set up out of the crate is probably not going to be ideal for your body type, reach, hands, legs, and preferred riding posture. But there are several adjustments you can make with just a few ordinary tools and your owner's manual.

Start with the most important components on the bike: the primary controls. These are the bike's puppet strings that make it turn, stop, and go: handlebars, brake lever, throttle grip, clutch lever, shift lever, and brake pedal.

Put the bike on the centerstand or garage stands and have a seat. If you don't have a centerstand, buy a 12-pack of beer and invite a couple of helpers over to hold the bike up while you sit on it. Assume your standard riding position. This should include your head and eyes up and searching the horizon, your back straight, your arms and elbows relaxed, your hands relaxed and on the handgrips, your knees tight against the bike, and your feet planted on the footrests or floorboards. Your knees should be bent too, for leverage, and not stretched out onto overlong forward controls.

Your hands should find the handgrips somewhere about mid-chest-level and shoulder-width apart, with your elbows bent 30 to 60 degrees. This angle works best because it provides the most leverage at the handlebars for precise and efficient steering. If your handlebars put your hands too high, too low, too close, too far away, or at awkward angles, adjust or replace them. If you don't fix these things now, they will come back to affect

accommodate any shortcomings the bike still may have. And as the bike (and your body) ages, things start to loosen up, and you'll find yourself adapting a little more and more every year to wrest the same performance out of the same machine(s).

Ideally, the perfect bike should fit you like a glove and be set up for the type of riding you do, so this chapter is about baselining, modifying, and maintaining your bike so it's always in tiptop shape and ready to take on the world.

Adjusting the Controls

Off the showroom floor, bikes are set up for everybody. That is, everybody who's exactly a five-foot-nine, 190-pound

Your fingers should reach straight out or slightly down to find the clutch and brake levers. The lever should generally be on the same plane as your forearm.

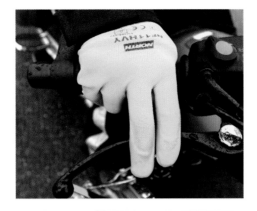

The distance from the bar to the lever should be close enough that you can curl the outer digits of your fingertips over the lever without actually engaging the lever.

your control somehow or somewhere later on down the road.

Now try the front brake and clutch levers. When your arms and hands are comfortable with the reach to the bars, you should have a natural and comfortable reach to the levers from the grips. Adjusting the levers up and down is simple enough, just loosen the bracket and rotate the lever up or down to your liking. Many bikes have in-out adjustable levers as well, so if the reach is too far or not far enough, you can change the angle of the lever to improve your finger-reach. If your bike does not

have in-out adjustable levers, you may be able to source levers from another bike or from the aftermarket that fit your hand size better.

You should also adjust the throttle and clutch mechanisms, if possible — especially if your bike is not showroom-new. Refer to your owner's manual for these adjustments. Each should have about a quarter-inch of "freeplay," or wiggle room, to work best. This means the clutch lever at rest (all the way out) should be able to move just slightly toward the handlebars without any resistance. It should feel just a little

Some riders like this riding position, while others are more comfortable with their knees bent and their feet underneath them. Changing the location of the foot controls can be expensive, so it's best to start with a bike that has the footrests more or less where you want them.

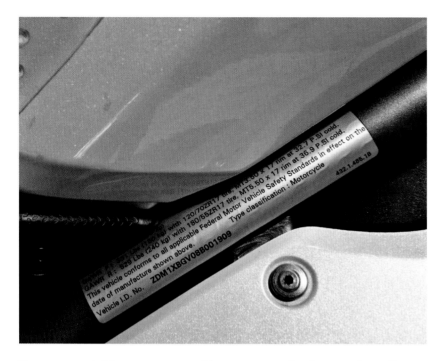

The recommended tire pressures are cold pressures, meaning those are the readings you should get after the motorcycle has been sitting overnight, not after you've been riding all afternoon. It's best to ignore the pressure recommendations on the tire itself—those tires will fit any number of bikes. The bike manufacturer has already taken the tire manufacturer's recommendation into consideration and, in some cases, has even assisted the tire manufacturer in developing the tire for your particular bike. Remember that the bike-recommended pressures can be considered baseline settings: you have some wiggle room to adjust them more to your liking.

"loose," though only for a quarter-inch or so. The throttle should have the same freeplay. You should be able to rotate the throttle grip a quarter-inch without feeling any resistance from the cable or return spring. Having freeplay in both the throttle grip and clutch cable will improve your overall control and help you ride more smoothly.

Too much freeplay can cause problems too, so be careful not to over-adjust. A clutch lever with too much freeplay will never completely disengage the clutch when you squeeze it, which may give you shifting problems. A throttle grip with too much freeplay will give you unpredictable throttle control, and the herky-jerky result will be unnerving to the rider . . . though hilarious to onlookers.

Next, move on to the secondary adjustments: the handgrips, footrests,

and seat. If your hands are larger or smaller than what the manufacturer decided they should be, it's easy enough to buy a different set of grips to mount on your handlebars to give you better feel and control. Softer, stickier grips can help with an aggressive riding style or allow you to be a little more comfortable on daylong rides. We don't recommend adding a throttle lock or cruise control on a motorcycle for safety reasons. "Cruise control" is something meant for cars and long trips on the freeway. Riders should always be ready to roll on or roll off in a bad situation.

Footrests and seats are generally pretty expensive, and it's hard to know just what will work for you and your bike. Model-specific clubs and Internet forums are good places to learn what changes riders have made to their bikes and how they worked out. Footrests can benefit from special mounting systems to move them up, down, forward, or backward to give you the exact riding position you want. You may also want to convert your ordinary footpegs to floorboards instead. An aftermarket seat can do wonders for your comfort and feeling of control, but again, seats can be kind of expensive, and the purchase may require you to send your bike's seat away to have it modified. Find out what other riders of your size and weight are using on their bikes to help you make your decision.

Tire Pressure

Getting your tire pressure just right for you, your bike, and your riding style is an often overlooked bike-setup adjustment. Lots of riders just leave the tires at the pressures the bike had when they bought it—literally. They never check the tire pressure, ever. Other riders, a little more conscientious about their tires, will at least make a monthly effort to keep the tire pressures at the bike manufacturer's recommended settings.

If you don't care about tire pressures at all and don't want to monkey with them, the manufacturer's settings are just fine. There is undoubtedly a lot of research done to determine what the optimal pressures are for comfort, stability, grip, and control. Look in the owner's manual or for a sticker on the bike that tells you what the (cold) pressures should be. Remember to adjust the tire pressures from these settings if you're dealing with temperature extremes or carrying a passenger.

But what if you're a rider who wants more say in what tire pressures you're running? Do you have to stick with the manufacturer's recommendation? Of course not. You can adjust these pressures a few pounds up or down from their OEM operating range. Doing this can make the ride harder or softer, give you better turning feel or better straight-line feel, or give you better grip or increased wear. Generally speaking, the higher the pressure, the harder the ride will be, the bike will be easier to turn, the tires will wear slower, and their operating temperature will be a bit cooler. Lower pressures will soften the ride, make the bike a little more sluggish when turning, increase tire wear and make them run hotter. But beware: underinflation is the surest way to learn about catastrophic tire failure. Don't deviate *too* far from the manufacturer's recommendations.

To find your optimal tire pressure for your riding style and your bike, start with the manufacturer's settings as your baseline and ride it for a couple of weeks, noting things like the plushness of the ride, how easily the bike turns in low- and high-speed corners, and how well the tires feel like they're gripping the road. Decide what, if any, of these ride characteristics you'd like to change, and change the pressures only 1 psi at a time—don't deviate more than 10 or 15 percent from the manufacturer's recommendation.

For example, if you want to soften your ride, lower the pressures by 1 psi each, then go for a ride and see what you think. If you like the change and want an even softer ride, lower them by another 1 psi and try it again.

> **"If you don't care about tire pressures at all and don't want to monkey with them, the manufacturer's settings are just fine."**

For everyday street use, these similar bikes may require different tire pressure settings, and the settings may be vastly different from those for a different style of motorcycle. The sportbike rider, for example, values increased grip over all else and is probably running something like 30 psi on the front and 28 on the rear. The touring bike rider, who is interested in long distances and infrequent tire replacement, is probably running more like 40 on the front and 42 on the rear. Neither setting is right or wrong; it just depends on what type of performance you want from your bike.

Another method of setting (or honing) tire pressure is to do it based on temperature. For optimal performance, a tire should feel almost (but not quite) hot when warmed up to operating temperature. The pressures you set to achieve this may need to change from season to season, as the air and the ground get warmer or colder.

Eventually, you'll reach a point in the plushness that makes the bike feel sluggish in turns, so you'll stop there or maybe add 1 psi to get you back to the pressure you liked just before you made the last change.

Similarly, if you want to make the bike turn a little quicker or easier, raise the pressures 1 psi and go for a ride. If you like what you feel, raise them another 1 psi and try it out. Keep playing with your tire pressures until you have them exactly where you want them in terms of comfort and feel. You can also change the tire pressure in one tire differently from the other, depending on what you're trying to accomplish. If you want longer wear on the rear but good grip on the front, for example, you can decrease the pressure 1 psi on the front and increase the pressure 1 psi on the rear. Play with these pressures for a month or more until you finally believe you have them all sorted out.

Okay, you've got your "mental" pressures set—the ones you set based on the way the bike feels to you. Take a final measurement of each tire's cold pressure and write it down. This is your personal baseline that you can revert back to anytime you want. Could we stop there? Sure. But we don't have to. There are still ways to increase our tires' performance through pressure settings.

Now, take a look at—or, rather, a feel of—the "physical" effects of pressure. Get out on your bike and ride it somewhat hard, turning corners as well as riding at freeway speeds. Get those tires up to operating temperature. From cold, this will take you at least 20 minutes of continuous riding on a warm day. When you've got the tires warmed up, quickly park the bike, take off your riding gloves, and immediately feel the tire treads. How's the temperature? For ideal grip and operating temperature, the tires should feel hot to the touch

When your bike is loaded up or you're carrying a passenger, you'll want to add some pressure to the tires to accommodate the weight. When you decide on the optimal passenger-carrying pressure, write that down too. *Kawasaki Motors Corp.*

but not so hot you can't hold your hand there. If you have to yank your hand away because a tire is too hot, raise the pressure 1 psi. If a tire doesn't feel pleasantly warm/borderline hot, or is cool to the touch, lower it by 1 psi. (If you're not parked back in your driveway, bring a hand or foot pump and tire gauge along with you.)

Then go ride for 20 more minutes and repeat the process. Keep adjusting each tire up or down until, after 20 minutes of riding, each tire is at the perfect temperature. Once you get to this point, check the new pressures first thing the next morning and write them down. This is your optimal baseline, and it's probably going to be different from your personal baseline . . . though it may resemble the manufacturer's recommended settings.

You and your bike's ideal tire pressures are going to be somewhere between your personal and optimal pressure settings. Now go back and use the first process again, riding the bike to feel for the plushness of the ride, how easily the bike turns in low- and high-speed corners, and how well the tires feel like they're gripping the road.

Adjust the pressures again to your liking, but only when the tires are cold, and be sure to stay within both your personal and optimal settings.

Once you've got your final pressures established, measure them cold and write them down, noting the air temperature that day too. If you live in a climate where air temperature changes from season to season, you'll want to repeat the entire process when the weather changes so you have both cold-weather settings and warm-weather settings. Check your tire temperatures after different types of riding, such as hard cornering at a track day or long stints in the saddle on a cross-country trip, and adjust as necessary. When you're back to your normal riding, you've got your baselines written down so you can easily revert back the next morning when the tires are cold again.

"Once you've got your final pressures established, measure them cold and write them down, noting the air temperature that day too."

> **"Now, there's an easy way to do this and an *enthusiastic* way to do this. We recommend the enthusiastic way, naturally."**

Suspension Theory and Baseline Setup

With all this talk about controls and tire pressures out of the way, it's time to dig in to the more mysterious side of bike setup: baselining your suspension. Your suspension components are what keep your tires in constant contact with the road for maximum control. Setting them up properly so the shock and fork springs put out just the right amount of pressure (preload and rate), and the fluids and valves control the springs' movement (compression and rebound damping), will be a huge benefit to you down the road. There are many excellent resources out there to give you expert knowledge of tuning and adjusting your own suspension, such as Kent Larson's *Track Day Handbook*. Setting your suspension's "sag" is a rather technical and involved process that is beyond the scope of this book. What follows will be a basic overview of suspension setup.

Now, there's an easy way to do this and an *enthusiastic* way to do this. We recommend the enthusiastic way, naturally. However, if you don't want to mess around with your suspension settings before you can go ride, just set them to the middle of their adjustment range and be done with it. On a big bike you can get away with this because the bike is so much heavier than the rider. (Not so much on a sportbike or racebike, where the rider's weight is closer to the bike's weight, and suspension tuning is paramount.) Check your owner's manual to determine exactly what adjusters exist on your bike, put them in the middle of their range, and leave them there. That should get you about where you need to be on a relatively new bike. On an older bike with a sacked-out suspension, all bets are off. If you ever develop a problem with your riding or bike that you suspect is a suspension problem, a quick conversation with a knowledgeable rider or suspension tuner can give you an idea which adjuster to turn or what component to replace.

Dialed In:
Suspension Setup the Enthusiastic Way

Do not be embarrassed if you are unfamiliar with the basics. Many experienced riders are. This is one reason some riders struggle with motorcycle control for years and never improve. If your bike isn't set up properly, it may frighten you, and you will assume that you are riding the best you can with only a small margin of safety. In the meantime, some of your friends just continue to go faster and improve while you stagnate. You can change this. Don't ride around handling problems, fix them. Sometimes it's as easy as turning a couple of screws.

There are four rules for tuning your own suspension. First, take your time. You know how long it took you to find the perfect tire pressures? That only involved one type of adjustment on each tire. Suspensions can have three or more possible adjustments for each wheel, so expect this to take some time. Next, don't be afraid to experiment. You shouldn't go turning knobs willy-nilly, of course, but trying different settings just to see what will happen is a good way to learn about suspension. Third, adjust only one thing at a time. Life is simpler when you can revert back to your last setting without having to guess what did what. Last, and

What does this knob do, and why would I want to turn it? Tuning your suspension for your weight and riding style is another way to take control of your bike and your riding ability.

Once you have your baseline settings down and are in the process of tuning your suspension to get exactly the handling and feel you want, remember to adjust only one thing at a time: fork spring preload, damping, or rebound *or* rear shock preload, damping, or rebound. If you turn a bunch of knobs at once, you may not know exactly which adjustment did what.

most important, take notes, not only for your day-to-day tuning, but also to look back in time when you've got a problem you're trying to solve.

The Rear Shock

The first and most basic adjustment is to set the "sag" on the shock, which means measuring and adjusting the spring to the middle of its range of up-and-down travel. This is done by adjusting the spring's preload, or in some cases, replacing the spring entirely with something softer (for lighter riders) or harder (for heavier riders). You'll need three or four burly friends and a promise of decent beer afterward for this project.

You measure sag by measuring the amount of up-and-down travel in the shock. Pick two fixed points on the rear of your bike: one on the rear of the swingarm and one on the subframe or bodywork above your point on the swingarm. First, find the fully extended measurement between your two points. Put the bike on

the centerstand, jack it up, or have your friends help you by lifting the bike to extend the rear suspension fully. Record the distance in millimeters at "full extension" in your notes.

Now take the bike off of its stand and balance it. *Push down* on the back of the bike, compressing the shock, and very slowly release it. Have another helper measure and record the distance.

Most bikes have at least a shock preload adjuster. This mechanism compresses the spring and can be adjusted to give you a harder or softer ride, or to react differently to bumps in the road.

Measuring your sag involves a lot of heavy lifting while you're seated on the bike with all your riding gear on, and it also involves some trial and error to get your sag set just right. Get a few friends together, plan to do everybody's bike, and make a day of it.

Now have a helper or three *lift* the rear of the bike up and let it settle down very slowly, then measure again. Halfway between the these two measurements is the measurement you want. Subtract that number from your full extension number, and that's your "free sag."

The next measurement is rider sag. Take the bike off of its stand, sit on it with your feet on the pegs and all your riding gear on, and have your helpers balance it. Have one helper push down on the back of the bike, compressing the shock, and very slowly release it. Measure the distance again. Now have your helpers lift the bike to top it out (yes, you are on the bike, and yes, this is very heavy) and let it settle very slowly, and take another measurement. Find the average of the two numbers again and subtract from your original full-extension measurement. This is your rear rider sag measurement. You should have about 25mm of sag.

This is your baseline rear shock setting and can be adjusted by changing the preload. If you have too much rider sag (more than 30mm), add preload to the spring. If you have too little rider sag

(less than 20mm), soften the preload.

Now you need to set the damping. The object is to get the suspension to respond as quickly as possible to irregularities in the pavement. Damping controls the speed at which the spring moves.

Set your rebound damping adjuster first. It is usually located at the bottom of your rear shock. As you push on the seat, the spring should return quickly but not instantaneously. It should take approximately one second for it to return to the top from a hard push. You should be able to watch the seat rise, as if controlled. If it just pops back up, you need to add rebound. If it drags up slowly, loosen it up. If you have a compression adjuster on your shock, it is located on the reservoir. Set it up in the middle of its range. You can determine how to adjust it after your test ride.

The Fork

You use the same basic process to set the sag in your fork. First you need a fully extended measurement. It's been said that the only way to get this measurement with any consistency is to lift from the handlebars until the front wheel actually leaves the ground. Measure the exposed area of the fork slider and write it down. On a conventional fork, this will be from the bottom of the lower triple clamp to the top of the dust seal on the lower slider. For an inverted or "upside down" fork, this will be from the dust seal down to the top edge of the aluminum axle clamp.

Follow the exact same measurement procedures with the fork as you did on the shock. The sag measurement you're looking for is about 35mm of rider sag. The front fork has to have more sag so that the front wheel may move down into a hole as well as up and over a bump. If your fork has too much sag (more than 45mm), increase the preload. If it has too little (less than 25mm), decrease the preload. If you don't have preload adjusters, then you will have to remove your forks and install different preload spacers.

Next is the damping adjustment. The fork needs to move much faster than the shock. Again, you should be able to watch it rebound but not as slowly as the shock. Start with the adjusters in the middle of their range. Grab the front brake and push down on the front of the bike as hard as you can. Observe its rebounding action. You want it to rise as quickly as possible without topping out and settling back down again. Loosen the rebound adjuster until the bike *does* want to settle back after topping out, and then dial in just enough rebound to make that settling tendency go away. The compression adjuster should be set as softly as possible but should prevent the fork from bottoming over severe bumps or under hard braking.

If you do not have these adjusters available to you externally, then you must change your fork oil weight to adjust the damping. Thicker oil affects both compression and rebound damping, but it primarily affects rebound damping. Thicker oil increases the damping, while thinner oil will decrease damping. If your forks work properly over bumps but bottom under hard braking, you can add more oil or "raise the level" to help prevent bottoming.

The Ride

Now that you have a good baseline setup, it's time for a test ride. Ensure that your tires have your favorite pressure in them, and head out for a ride. There are several things you need to analyze as you ride:

Keep your tools handy so you can make adjustments to front or rear suspension when you're away from home.

Some guys think it's cool to drag stuff through corners. It ain't. If you lean in hard enough on a bike to scrape parts, you'll lift a tire off the ground . . . and immediately take its place on the pavement! In other words, this is serious business.

Stability. Go fast in a straight line, and your bike should never scare you.

Cornering performance. What is the overall stability, steering effort, ground clearance, front wheel action, and rear wheel action? The main things to look for here are wallowing and spongy action. There shouldn't be any. Wallow indicates a need for a higher spring rate. Note whether you have to work to keep the bike on your cornering line. If you have anything dragging on the ground, you have a problem that could result in injury. Get the dragging stuff up and out of the way, preferably, or change the ride height. Remember that changing ride height will alter the bike's basic handling characteristics.

Front wheel action. The wheel should roll smoothly through the corner and inspire confidence. If the wheel is bouncing, and you can't really feel it in the bars, then this is a lack of rebound damping. If the handlebars are jarring you, then you may have too much spring preload or compression damping. Use rebound damping carefully. Too much rebound damping creates a situation where the fork is "packing down." This means your fork has collapsed and is not re-extending fast enough. You need to speed up your rebound damping or raise the fork oil level, or use more compression damping to keep the fork from bottoming.

Rear wheel action. If your bike feels like a "pogo stick," then this is typically an all-around lack of damping. Be careful about using too much rebound damping, as with the fork. Too much rebound will cause the rear wheel to "swim" under the bike during hard straight-line braking because the shock is packing up and the rear wheel is hanging up instead of returning to the ground. A lack of compression damping will cause the bike to pogo while under acceleration. This will be a vertical "sawing" motion. Too much compression damping will make the bike "buck" or kick you in the butt over sharp bumps.

Remember, as you adjust your suspension, adjust only one thing at a time. That way, if you don't like the change you just made, you can change it back and try something else. And don't bite off more than you can chew. This is only a basic introduction to suspension adjustment. If you really want to get into it, you'll need a little more book learnin', and maybe an expert tuner, to do it right. Last, if you want to cheat, just copy what someone else with your same build and bike is

If you own a popular bike, odds are there's a club or Internet forum you can join to find out what tires, pressures, suspension settings, and aftermarket controls and suspension components other people are running. If figuring out your own suspension settings bores you to tears, you can always cheat and use someone else's who has the same build and bike you have. *Kawasaki Motors Corp.*

A motorcycle rider uses his or her whole body to ride smoothly and skillfully. Many riders subconsciously hold onto the bike by the handlebars, especially when they're tired or stressed by a riding situation. *Don't do that.* You should hold onto those handlebars like you're holding onto a pair of baby birds. Your best riding will come when you're holding on with your lower body and your upper body is relaxed and ready to react at a moment's notice. *Yamaha Motor Corp.*

doing—provided they've taken all the time to do all this stuff and know what they're talking about.

To truly dial your bike in to your particular riding style and physical characteristics, setting the sag is not an option, it's a requirement. Setting the sag establishes the perfect baseline upon which to make all future suspension adjustments. Most riders can get by without setting the sag on their motorcycles, or even knowing what

the term "sag" means. But for those trying to achieve maximum control, it's a piece of the puzzle that should not be left out.

The Most Important Setup of All

None of these bike setup adjustments are going to help you one whit if your riding posture sucks. I kid you not—riders 10 times our skill level are amazed at what simple, correct posture does for their big-bike control.

Proper body position is the foundation from which all the skills in this book will be built. You should have your shoulders relaxed, arms loose, a light, firm grip on the handlebars, back straight, knees pressed tightly against the motorcycle, balls of the feet on the footpegs or feet planted solidly on the floorboards, and head up and eyes up and focused on the horizon. Don't leave your driveway without a quick review of good posture. And every time you're having trouble with a particular skill, stop and do a posture check: shoulders, arms, hands, back, knees, feet, head, and eyes.

While the authors don't endorse this riding *ensemble*, notice how relaxed this rider's upper body is. He's not fighting the bike at all through the turn, he's got it steered, and he's merely guiding it with a good head turn and light touch on the bars.

The Friction Zone

■ **Zero to One Hundred in Three Inches**
■ **Coordinated Fine-Muscle Control**

The friction zone, while not quite the twilight zone, is not too far from it. It is an odd place that we don't often think to visit, but for maximum control of a big bike, it is a place with which we have to become intimately familiar to keep our relationships with our bikes easy and comfortable.

Simply put, the friction zone is a position of your clutch lever that's somewhere between fully squeezed and fully released. But this position, or rather, this range of possible positions, is the last word in controlling your big bike at low speeds. I know, I know, it sounds a little basic; you want to get on to the fun stuff, but bear with us.

You're going to have a lot of trouble with Chapters 3, 4, and 5 if you don't pay your dues to Chapter 2. Mastering the friction zone is the Holy Grail of low-speed riding and critical to overall control of your heavyweight motorcycle.

First, let's make sure we're clear. When we talk about low-speed riding, we're talking about moving at less than 10 miles per hour with your feet off the ground and on the pegs or floorboards. At these speeds, you have to turn the motorcycle by physically turning the handlebars, rather than leaning the bike first by countersteering (discussed in Chapter 5). Countersteering still works at these speeds, but the inputs

Riding a motorcycle at high speed is easy. It's riding it at low speed that really takes skill and finesse. *Yamaha Motor Corp.*

Opposite: You've got to learn to walk before you can learn to run. Being able to throw your heavyweight bike around like a pro requires masterful use of the friction zone, as well as coordinated fine-muscle control of the clutch and throttle. Most riders think they know how to use the friction zone, but rarely do they ever practice it—which is why most riders have a hard time with the tight stuff.

Clutch fully squeezed = 0 percent power to the wheel. Remember, squeezing the clutch is the same as shutting the engine off.

Clutch fully released = 100 percent power to the wheel. The bike is now controlled with throttle grip.

Somewhere between fully squeezed and fully released lies the ever-elusive friction zone—the zone in which the engine transmits only a portion of the engine's power to the rear wheel. You now control the bike using the muscles in your left hand to make small, smooth, and precise adjustments of the clutch while simultaneously using the muscles in your right hand to make small, smooth, and precise inputs to the throttle.

are so subtle that most riders don't feel it. Of course you can still lean the motorcycle, but in order to get a direction change you are going to have to have the handlebars turned. This means low-speed riding is a little more "labor intensive." Why don't we use this as our general description for riding slow: low-speed riding means you have to turn the handlebars physically to keep the motorcycle balanced in order to turn the motorcycle.

The next thing we have to be clear about is how you know you're in low-speed control of the motorcycle. You can tell when you're in control because the motorcycle is moving smoothly through whatever action you're taking, whether it is slow, smooth, straight-ahead riding or a slow U-turn that starts from a stop at an intersection. Sitting on the motorcycle, you're relaxed in your arms and shoulders, you feel confident in what you are doing, and it's obvious to anybody watching that you're confident in yourself and in your actions.

Zero to One Hundred in Three Inches

Using the friction zone is all about coordinated fine-muscle control of the clutch and throttle. This means that you are using the muscles in your left hand to make small, smooth, and precise adjustments of the clutch while simultaneously using the muscles in your right hand to make small, smooth, and precise inputs to the throttle.

You'll find the friction zone using the clutch lever. With the bike running and in gear, if you keep the clutch lever squeezed, you're transmitting zero power to the rear wheel. As you ease the lever out, the friction zone begins at the point where the clutch starts to grab and pull the motorcycle forward. In other words, it is the point where the clutch just begins to transfer energy to the rear wheel. The friction zone ends when the clutch is fully released and 100 percent of the engine's power is being transferred to the rear wheel.

What interests us is the useful part of that friction zone, the part between that 1 and 100 percent. As you release that clutch, the lever moves some small distance, maybe a few inches, to get from 1 to 100 percent power transfer. Here is where that fine-muscle control comes in; you have to be able to squeeze or release that clutch in tiny increments in order to get into the optimum power band, greater than 1 percent, less than 100 percent. Just exactly where that optimum power band is depends on many factors, and every bike/rider combo is different. However, it's safe to say that you want to be somewhere between 25 and 75 percent of the available power going to the rear wheel. Does this sound familiar? What you are doing is what is also known as "slipping" the clutch.

I know what some of you are thinking: what the heck are these guys

Friction Zone Tip Number 1
CLUTCH CONTROL

Get all four fingers around that clutch lever. When the lever is fully extended, all of your fingers may not quite reach, but that's okay—they will once you start squeezing. This is not racing, this is not showing off, this is about fine-muscle control, and it works best with all four fingers working that clutch lever.

talking about? Slipping the clutch? No way, that's just nuts. I've been driving a stick-shift car, truck, or big rig for years, and slipping the clutch ruins it. Well, you are absolutely right, slipping the clutch on a car, truck, or big rig does ruin it. But on a motorcycle the clutch plates are "wet." There's a thin sheet of oil between them, and they're *meant* to be slipped. Slipping a clutch on a motorcycle is part of what the motorcycle was designed to do. (Well, most motorcycles. There are some that use a dry clutch. Dry clutches don't age as gracefully when slipped as wet clutches do. Fortunately for our discussion,

Friction Zone Tip Number 2
THROTTLE CONTROL

Just like with the clutch, the best fine-muscle control for the throttle comes with all four fingers wrapped around that throttle control and your wrist bent gently downward. Not just one or two fingers resting on that front brake lever but all four fingers around the throttle will give you the best control. However, if your hands

are truly more like hams and you have trouble with smooth throttle control using all four fingers, it's okay to hold the throttle with one or two fingers. That is, use your thumb and first two fingers at the very least, but your pinkie and ring fingers can hang off the end of the bar.

Riding Drill Number 1
WALK THE LINE

Find an empty parking lot with a long, straight line you can follow. Mark off 110 feet. Ride as slowly as you can, following the line. Adjust your clutch and throttle inputs to get that engine turning liquid smooth. Keep your head up and your eyes on the horizon, then use your inner ear and peripheral vision to orient you to the line.

Once you find a good combination of clutch and throttle, drop your speed a little. Find the new sweet spot, and continue dropping your speed until you're floating along at barely a walking pace. You are not going to find this sweet spot at first. You are going to have to make the necessary coordinated fine clutch and throttle adjustments as you practice and get the feel for what you're doing. Give yourself time to develop this skill.

Practice this for 20 minutes a day, three days a week. Within a few weeks you should be able to walk a 110-foot line in 25 seconds or more. Once you feel you've mastered your friction zone and are able to walk the line in 20 seconds or more, you only need to practice the drill once a month for 20 minutes.

You can also practice this any time you're stuck in traffic, in a parking lot, or even just coming up to a stop. Walk the line smoothly while traffic is busy stopping and going. Walk the line while trolling for a parking place at the mall. And walk the line as you approach the last few stop signs on your route home from work. Of course, make sure traffic is clear behind you and you aren't holding anybody up.

Extra credit. Practice this for a few minutes at the beginning and end of each ride. Have patience. This is not something that is going to come easy, and you're going to have to work at it. So keep working at it every time you ride to keep it sharp.

110 ft.

10 Seconds: 7.5 MPH

20 Seconds: 3.75 MPH

30 Seconds: 1.875 MPH

30 feet, 7 seconds

60 feet, 14 seconds

90 feet, 21 seconds

most big bikes use a wet clutch.) If your moto-conscience still won't let you "slip" the clutch, you might try to fake it out by using the more masculine and multipurpose term "feather" the clutch. Both terms mean the same thing when it comes to the clutch.

Coordinated Fine-Muscle Control

So you're in your friction zone, let's say at 50 percent power. I am sure we all know, or have figured out by now, that you can't just slip the clutch to get the motorcycle to move forward. While you're releasing the clutch you also have to give the bike a little gas by twisting on the throttle. If you don't, of course, the motorcycle will stall. But do you use the throttle like an on/off switch? Hell no. You use the same approach to the throttle as you use with the clutch—adjusting your right hand in tiny increments to measure out exactly the amount of gas that's needed. Instead of thinking of throttle management as rolling on, rolling off, and steady throttle, think of it in the more subtle terms of positive, negative, and neutral twisting pressure on the throttle grip. Even one millimeter at the handgrip can make a difference in the way your bike behaves. Keep your wrist "down" rather than "up" to improve your throttle control (see side-view photo in Friction Zone Tip Number 2).

Now we return to the coordinated element of fine-muscle control we mentioned earlier. While you're releasing the clutch a sliver at a time to get power to the rear wheel, you are also varying the pressure with which you're twisting the throttle grip. You're mixing and matching the inputs to get the bike to behave like you want. But how much clutch and throttle do you need? Depends. Every bike is different. Every rider is different. Every maneuver that requires coordinated fine-muscle control is different. It's up

This rider is listening to the bike and feeling what it's doing. He's not worried about his speed or rpm.

"Remember to always let your bike help you. Listen to what your engine is telling you. Feel what the bike is telling you."

to you to practice this enough so that you'll always have a perfect and familiar combination of clutch and throttle at your fingertips whenever you need it. Remember to always let your bike help you. Listen to what your engine is telling you. Feel what the bike is telling you. If you do this you will always know when you have everything right.

A word of advice: do not overthink this. Let's look at an example. Say that you have found a sweet spot that happens to be at the 30 percent point of your friction zone. You also find that if you give it 10 percent positive throttle and get it up to 3,500 rpm, your big bike moves smoothly through any maneuver you try. Theoretically, you could open the clutch up to 70 percent power and drop the engine rpms down to 3,000 and achieve exactly the same amount of smoothness. However, the reality

is you are working with such minute adjustments in the clutch and throttle that you're better off listening to your engine, feeling what it's doing, and then working from there. Ignore the gauges, go by feel. One time the engine rpms may be a little higher than they were the last time, or your throttle position might be slightly different. But if you're in control and you like the way it feels, just go with it.

How do you tell when your clutch and throttle combination is just right? You'll hear your engine purring along at a nice, even rpm, and everything on the motorcycle will be balanced just right. It's all a very subtle, highly choreographed dance between you, the clutch, and the throttle. And, just like anything that's highly choreographed, the only way to keep it perfect is to get all the players together and rehearse.

Chapter 3
The Friction Zone Part Two

▌ **Sound and Feel**
▌ **The Dreaded U-Turn**

Previous page: When you are out riding your motorcycle at speed, which is most of the time, sensing what the engine is doing is not something you think about much. You mostly use your eyes and inner ears to sense speed, position, and motion. But when you slow down to three, four, or five miles per hour, it's your butt that's going to tell you a lot about what is happening with your motorcycle.

"So, keep your eyes where you want to go and let your motorcycle tell you what you need to do through your ears and your butt."

Friction Zone Tip Number 3
STAY OFF THAT FRONT BRAKE!

In very low-speed turns, you have to stay off of the front brake. Too much, or sometimes any, front brake during a slow turn will cause the bike to drop into the inside. At low speeds, this will usually mean a tip-over. If you have to brake during a low-speed, tight turn of any kind, use the rear brake only. Let us say that again: *Do not use that front brake!* For any braking or slowing, use the rear brake only.

Okay, let's take a moment here to let you in on a major motorcycle secret. It's rarely discussed out in the open, more often it's overheard between two experienced riders, in the back of motorcycle shops or in the pits of a racetrack or training circuit. It's not mentioned in any of the training courses (except maybe for the ones in which *we're* doing the talking), and it's not written in any books. In fact, this may be the first time that anybody has taken the time to talk about this obscure subject in public: there are a couple of other personal skills associated with riding a motorcycle using the friction zone and knowing when you are in control. These skills involve *sound* and *feel*.

Listen! I know when you're riding you listen to the sounds of traffic around you, but you also have to listen to the sound of your motorcycle engine, especially when you are riding slowly. Does it sound smooth and even? If it does, then the rear wheel is getting the power it needs to keep you moving. Or is it starting to chugalug down in the rpms? If this is the case, then that rear wheel needs more power, and you had better do something quick to get it what it wants. If you don't, the motorcycle will stall, and at low speed this can mean trouble.

Feel! When you are riding your motorcycle, where do you think you mostly sense what your engine is doing? Is this something you've ever even considered? Is that first sense of feeling your hands? No. How about your feet? No. Then where?

Think about it. Imagine accelerating up to speed, or bringing the bike down to speed for a turn, and deciding what gear to choose. What part of your body gives you the real feel for what your engine is doing? If you answered your butt, you were right. Right there in your butt, baby, there is where you get the first, best, and most feeling of just what is going on with that motorcycle beneath you.

What we are trying to say here is that riding that big bike in the friction zone means you have to really pay attention to your senses. You have to listen to and feel the vibes from the engine to make sure it's running smoothly enough to handle what you are doing. You have to feel how the bike is moving under you to make sure you can make whatever minor adjustment you need to keep your balance. So, keep your eyes where you want to go and let your motorcycle tell you what you need to do through your ears and your butt. Most importantly, let your motorcycle do all of the work! Have faith in yourself, in the skills you are going to learn and practice, and in your machine.

The Dreaded U-Turn
The next step in getting a solid hold on the friction zone is practicing your U-turns in both directions. This is one

of the hardest things for many people to do on any size of a motorcycle, but it is especially difficult with big bikes. The tighter the turn you want, the more you have to work the bike—and at low speeds, a mistake usually ends up with the bike and rider on the ground. There's not enough forward motion to keep the bike stable. At slow, walking speeds, the bike is mostly upright. A leaned-over motorcycle requires a lot more friction zone control because the bike wants to fall, and you have to work to keep it from falling. That is, it wants to fall into the turn, and you have to use the friction zone to keep it from doing just that.

And for many people, yes, it is harder to turn to the right than it is to the left. There's plenty of speculation out there as to why this is the case, but the primary reason is your arms are each in a different position. In a turn, one arm will be bent and perhaps held tightly into your body, the other will be stretched out, perhaps farther than you're comfortable. However, you still need coordinated fine-muscle control, no matter what your different arms may be doing, in order to make the smooth, slow, controlled, sharp turns. And the

only way you're going to get this is through lots and lots of practice.

Practicing U-turns is not quite as easy as slow riding in a straight line. Making tight, controlled turns during everyday riding just does not happen all that much. This is probably why sharp turns and U-turns can be so hard for people. So here's your first piece of U-turn advice: when you start out on a ride and when you come home from a ride, practice U-turns for a few minutes on your quiet, residential street. That is, of course, if you live near a quiet, residential street where you can safely do this without interrupting traffic. If you don't have a street like this handy, find one, or find a quiet parking lot nearby.

Start out practicing U-turns using as much room as you need. At first, don't worry about your turning radius, don't even think about it. Just work on keeping that engine smooth and purring, coordinating your fine clutch and throttle muscles, measuring out just the right amount of power to the rear wheel, and keeping the motorcycle balanced throughout the turn.

The keys to masterful, low-speed U-turns at this point are keeping your

Although not as glamorous as a U-turn with parts of the bike dragging on the ground, the upright, tight U-turn gets the job done just as well without as much risk of falling.

Riding Drill Number 2
FIGURE EIGHT

An excellent practice drill is simply turning figure eights, which in reality are continuous U-turns in both directions. The tighter the figure eight, the better your skill. This exercise works both your steering arms (gross motor skills) and fine-muscle control simultaneously, which is not always easy to do. Be careful not to ride so long you get dizzy or disoriented. Once every few minutes, leave the area and breeze out your brain a little.

Start out with 10 times more space than you need. This means a big, wide, obstacle-free parking lot. Set up two cones 40

feet apart. (If at first you need them more than 40 feet apart, feel free to stretch them out. With enough practice, you'll have them down to 20 feet or less before you know it.) With the cones as your guide, start turning big, wide figure eights, keeping your body upright, the bike leaned beneath you, your arms steady, keeping your clutch and throttle in the friction zone.

Do these 40-foot, over-wide turns for however long it takes for you to get consistent and comfortable with it. Then, start making the U-turns a little tighter. Aim to ride as close to the

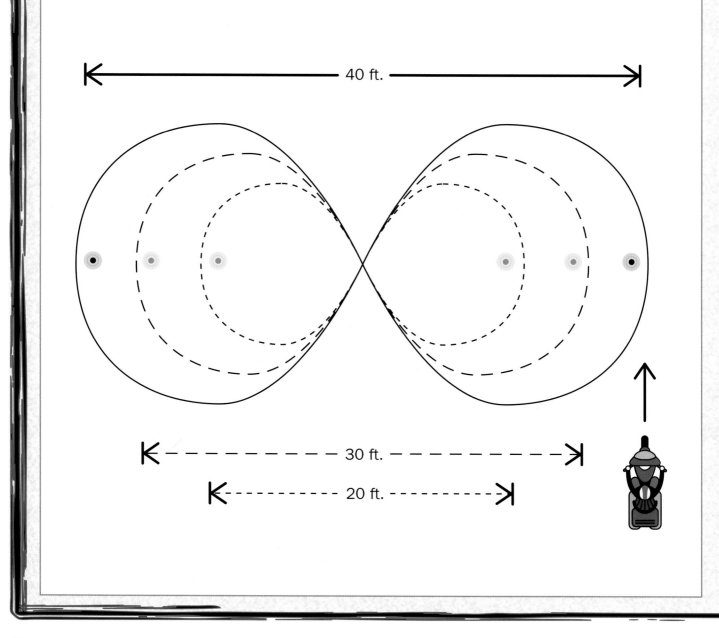

cones as you can. Once you get comfortable with this, you'll find you're making two tight U-turns with a little straight in between. That's when you know it's time to move the cones closer together. When 40 feet is a piece of cake, move them to 30. Your goal is ultimately to get the cones 20 feet apart or less, depending on what your bike can do, and when you get to the point where you're

making U-turns with the bars turned all the way to lock, you're now in the range of skill that the motorcycle cops have.

Remember: take it slow, take it easy, and be in control of the bike at every moment. This is not a race. This is learning and practice. You should practice this drill twice a month for one full hour.

1

When you initiate the turn, your head and eyes are focused on the opposite side of the cone; turn your head at least 90 degrees, and keep your eyes two to three seconds ahead.

2

When you're about halfway through the turn, your head and eyes are already looking toward the next turn; again, keep your head turned 90 degrees and focus your eyes two to three seconds up the road.

3

Three-quarters of the way through the turn, you've found your turn-in point for the next turn; keep your head and eyes 90 degrees turned and two to three seconds ahead.

4

Keep your body upright, weight the outside peg, keep your head turned 90 degrees, and keep your eyes level with the horizon. Note that this rider is dragging the rear brake for additional control and stability—an advanced technique.

It's totally okay when you first start learning U-turns if you need to walk through it before getting your feet up. You're still practicing coordinated fine-muscle control and a good head turn, without having to worry about dropping your bike. Sometimes in the real world you have to do this, if you get yourself into a tricky spot or are just having a bad day.

"In power-walking you are forced to use that front brake. This means that you have to use very light, very precise fine-muscle control on the front brake lever—if indeed you find yourself having to use it."

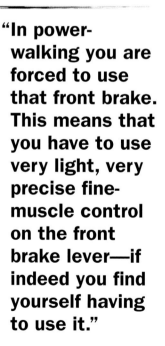

body upright, keeping the bike *mostly* upright and directly underneath you, and turning your head and eyes to look all the way through the turn. Note that the degree of lean and counterweighting also depends on the weight of the bike and how tightly you intend to turn. In low-speed turns, your balance and equilibrium will be better if you don't try to lean the bike too much. Leaning the bike at low speed is for when you have perfected your control of the friction zone because it requires you to counterbalance the bike. For now, you and the bike are both mostly upright, and you are focusing your head and eyes on where you want your bike to be, rather than where it is at the moment, which will help keep you smooth and balanced throughout the turn.

Once you have your body position, head turn, and friction zone under control, work on holding the handlebars steady throughout the turn. You don't want that awful "handlebar bounce." This is where you're constantly wiggling (or jerking) the handlebars back and forth to maintain balance. Use your friction zone to maintain your balance

instead. Practice getting those bars turned and holding them at the same angle from start to finish in the turn. (This is why we advise starting out with as much room as you need—it takes lots of repetition to outgrow the handlebar bounce.)

For whatever reason, maybe you're having a little bit of trouble working on the figure eights. They don't feel right, you don't have the control that you would like. Maybe you are having a hard time managing coordinated fine-muscle control with one arm stretched out and the other one tucked in. Or maybe you just want to see what a U-turn is like before you actually ride one. If this is the case, you can "power-walk" the figure eight. This means you're still sitting on the motorcycle and using all the correct techniques of the head turn, upright body, and friction zone, only you're walking along very slowly as you do it, using your feet for balance and keeping the motorcycle upright, not leaned into the turns.

There are two things to remember while power-walking. One, your right foot will be on the ground, so you won't

Friction Zone Tip Number 4
HOW TIGHT DOES THAT U-TURN HAVE TO BE?

If you have practiced to the point that you can do an entire U-turn with the handlebars completely locked, you have worked very hard, and you should be proud of the skill you have developed. But the reality is that in most cases, your average roadway will offer you about 30 feet to work with. This is just a little narrower than your average urban residential street. So being able to ride a U-turn with the handlebars locked is a great skill to have, but it's not necessary in most cases.

be able to use the cardinal "rear-brake-only" rule. In power-walking you are forced to use that front brake. This means that you have to use very light, very precise fine-muscle control on the front brake lever—if indeed you find yourself having to use it. Second, your turning radius will be much, much greater than if you were leaning the bike, so you may need a little more room. Don't let these big turns discourage you. Once you're into riding with your feet up and the bike leaned, your U-turn performance (radius) will be much tighter.

Let's make sure that we all understand something before we go any further. U-turns are tough. They're not something we see a lot in our daily riding. This means the only way you'll ever get good at it is to practice, whenever you have a chance. But remember, too, if you can make a slow, tight U-turn, then any other lesser turn will be a piece of cake.

Also, keep this in mind: there may come a time when you just can't hit your comfort zone, and you get yourself into that U-turn and you just can't make. This is No Big Deal. Don't

Remember what we said early on: practice at 100 percent, ride at 80 percent. Here's a good example why. Most roadways give you about 30 feet to work with. If you've practiced making U-turns at 20 feet, this big turn will be no problem for you.

When working in the friction zone, take frequent breaks and air yourself and your bike out a little. This will help keep the clutch plates cool and give your hands and concentration a rest.

force it—you'll just get yourself into trouble and most likely drop your big bike . . . and get more practice picking it up. Instead of risking it, if you see you're not going to make it, come to a smooth, controlled stop, using the rear brake only, and then do whatever it is you have to do (back up, power-walk) to finish the turn.

A Few Final Words

So, there you have it, smooth, controlled, slow riding on your big bike is all about getting that coordinated fine-muscle control between the clutch and throttle down. Listen to the engine and feel through your butt what the motorcycle is telling you. So is that all there is to it? Yes and no. You don't need to know any more than this to go out and slow ride with the best of them. You

practice, get it down, get comfortable with it, and you'll be covered. However, there is one other thing you can try.

After you get the coordinated fine-muscle control down between the clutch and the throttle so that you are riding both of this chapter's exercises comfortably and in control, you can try "riding" the rear brake. This is that little extra technique that motorcycle cops do to give them their phenomenal low-speed control of the bike. By adding the rear brake to the mix, you are now coming at the bike with coordinated fine-muscle control from three directions and are even better able to control your speed. Many riders of heavyweight bikes (and lightweight bikes, for that matter) use a variation of this technique for starting on a hill: if you hold the bike in place with your foot on the rear brake, it frees up your hands to find the friction zone and get the bike moving without rolling backward.

One last thing: when you practice friction zone maneuvers and spend a lot of time slipping your clutch, your bike (and your hands!) can get pretty heated up. Every now and then, take a moment just to ride around the block a couple of times. Breeze it out a little. You want to move some air past the engine so that you can keep the clutch plates cool. You want to move some air over your face and fingers too, so you stay fresh and focused.

Friction Zone Tip Number 5
TO LEAN OR NOT TO LEAN?

Getting into the friction zone sweet spot is what controls the motion of the bike at slow speed. Since your low-speed riding control is completely through the use of the friction zone, whether or not you lean while turning is completely up to you. It is your preference. If you want to keep the bike straight up and down, that works just fine. If you want to put a little lean into your turn, that works just fine too. It is your preference, and it's all about what works best for you to keep control of your big bike. The best thing we can suggest: go out riding and turning at low speed on your big bike and see what comes most naturally for you, then go with that.

Low-Speed Maneuvers

■ **Walking Control** ■ **Tight Turns**
■ **Turning from a Stop**

At low speeds, your big bike wants to find a place to lie down and rest. It's up to you and your skills to keep that from happening.

Previous page: Now we're going to put your friction zone skills to the test in the real world. Low-speed maneuvers in traffic are tricky on any bike but are especially tricky on a heavyweight bike. However, a little knowledge and practice go a long way to taking the mystery (and misery) out of this type of maneuver.

Because of a big bike's weight, low-speed riding becomes an important skill that needs to be practiced until perfect. When performing tight turns, making U-turns, and maneuvering at walking speeds, there's not enough forward motion to balance the motorcycle completely. The motorcycle has to be actively balanced by the rider. The motor-officer style of riding—clutch and throttle control while dragging the rear brake—is really meant for big bikes and slow speeds.

One common example of low-speed riding is in parking lots with a lot of traffic. The space available and speeds attainable are not quite fast enough for you to release the clutch completely and be engaged fully in gear. Low-speed riding conditions also occur during rush hours and stop-and-go freeway traffic or at stop signs or signal lights where there are a lot of vehicles that can move forward only a little bit at a time, taking turns moving through an intersection. Or there's fun stuff like riding in parades—always a good time but a lot of clutch and throttle work.

So, what amateur riders end up doing in all these situations is some type of partial clutch release and then a lot of coasting. And that's fine . . . for amateurs. But we know how to get this low-speed control by using the friction zone because we just spent the last two chapters discussing it. The friction zone is the key to controlling a big bike at low speeds, and it requires a good deal of practice to be any good at it.

Lowest Potential

The lowest possible potential for a motorcycle is a position where no further motion of any kind, in any direction, can occur. The first thought that comes to mind for lowest potential is when the motorcycle is stopped and is leaned over on its sidestand. Close, but not quite. You see, the sidestand can sink into soft asphalt, or the bike can be bumped from behind and fall over. Once it reaches this position, now it's at lowest potential. It no longer wants to move in any direction. Any motion whatsoever will require some kind of additional force.

The nature of the motorcycle beast being what it is, once the motorcycle gets moving forward faster than about 15 miles per hour, we don't have to work much to keep the motorcycle upright and stable. Our only job now in order to keep it upright is to keep it from running into something. As long as we do this, and don't reduce forward speed, the motorcycle will not fall to its lowest potential without an outside force.

Or, put another way, riding at low speeds is something we do frequently, and it provides multiple opportunities for your motorcycle to reach its lowest potential. This is especially true if you don't practice low-speed riding. Below 15 miles per hour, we have to work constantly at keeping the motorcycle balanced and upright.

Remember, whenever you are doing any slow riding and you have to stop, use your rear brake pedal only, or both front and rear brakes at the same time. In fact, stay away from the front brake entirely. In a slow-speed turning maneuver of any kind, a quick jab at the front brake with some rear brake will most likely put you down. So let's just make this easy: when slow riding, use only your rear brake to make it easy on yourself. In any case, if you have moved up to the optional top rung of the friction zone ladder, your foot is already riding that rear brake pedal.

Walking Control

Before we get to the good stuff, let's discuss the basics. No matter how good a rider you are, there comes a time when you have to move the motorcycle by pushing it, usually backward. Moving backward and looking over your shoulder to see where you're going while controlling the balance and speed of the motorcycle requires some skill—especially if you're trying to do it on an incline.

First things first: remember that it's not a race. Since this is a big piece of heavy machinery and you are completely controlling that weight from a relatively awkward, standing position, you must be slow and methodical with every step you take. And unfortunately for us, we can't adhere to the "rear brake only" rule of low speeds. It doesn't matter if you are pushing the bike or letting the bike roll backward downhill, if you get those handlebars turned too far and suddenly grab the front brake lever, you run the risk of dropping that bike. To make matters worse, you kind of *have* to use the front brake. Even a one-mile-per-hour bump can put a dent in a fender or car door or break the lens on your taillight. The only way ensure you don't drop your big bike is to be careful and calculated with that front brake lever.

Backing up a big bike is never, ever easy. Take it slow. Make sure of your footing. Look where you're going. Push with your legs. If you use these steps every time you have to move your big bike backward, chances are you will be able to keep the bike upright while you are moving it, and you will be able to put the bike where you want to the first time. None of this back-up, move-forward, back-up-again stuff.

As for walking your big bike forward, do it the same way. Don't

> **"The nature of the motorcycle beast being what it is, once the motorcycle gets moving forward faster than about 15 miles per hour, we don't have to work much to keep the motorcycle upright and stable."**

Wrong. This rider is trying too hard, is not focused on where he's going, and has no leverage. Worse yet, in this position, if the bike starts to go over, he's likely to get hurt trying to save it or get pinned underneath it.

struggle trying to use both handlebars, use one bar and some solid part of the bike for leverage and push with your legs. Or you can use the super-advanced, ultra-lazy method: let your bike do the work. Use the friction zone. (This comes in real handy when putting your bike up onto a lift or a ramp.) But beware when doing this; even though you are not using your muscles to push the bike, all of the things that apply to moving it backward apply to moving it forward. Always make sure of your footing and look where you're going. And remember, making a mistake with the clutch or losing your balance can have dire, dire consequences. Once again, slow, steady, and in control keeps you from having to pick that big bike up, hurting yourself, or hurting somebody else.

Tight Turns

Okay, here we go. Tight turns, in motor-cop lingo, are locked turns. While you are sitting still on your motorcycle sometime, turn the handlebars all the way to the right, then all the way to the left. They reach a point where they stop; they can't turn any more. That's the steer stop. Putting the handlebars into this stopped position and then

This is much better. The rider is using his upper body for balance and his legs for power, and his head and eyes are leading the way. Don't waste your energy twisting yourself all up and trying to drag the bike along by the handlebars. Find a good, solid place to push from and use your legs to move the bike. Taller riders find they have better control moving the bike around while straddling the seat. Be sure to use your legs for power rather than your arms and (gasp!) lower back.

As they say in the PGA, these guys are good. Hundreds of hours of frequent and focused training will do that for you. Skills like these are good to strive for, but we're going to focus on what we need to survive on the street. However, the techniques you'll learn in this book will lay the foundation for skills like this, if you do decide that this is your goal.

holding them there all the way through a turn is called a locked turn.

Since you can't turn the handlebars any farther, many think this is as sharp as you can turn the motorcycle, but it's not. You can lean that bike over and drag a board through a low-speed turn and turn that bike sharper than you ever thought possible. Needless to say this is some serious control of the friction zone and coordinated fine-muscle control.

Motorcycle cops go through 100 to 150 hours of training to learn and practice the friction zone so that they can ride like this, and only about half of those who start actually make it through the training. And then they hold organized practices for one day a month, or at the very least quarterly, and practice pretty much every day. They do 40-plus hours a week in the saddle, so they get a lot of time and opportunity to practice and work at what they do.

If you put that much time and practice in, you'd probably be able ride like motorcycle cops do; however, locked turns are an advanced technique that we are not going to worry about here. The only time we've ever had to use these techniques was during motor-officer training, and maybe once or twice in some heavy enforcement riding situations. As for average street riding, this is not a technique that we've had to use in 50-plus combined years of riding.

The key to tight turns, after getting the bars turned quickly and using the friction zone, is getting that head turned, eyes up, and looking to where you want to be. You cannot begin to imagine how much this simple step helps get you through that tight turn. It is so easy just to stare at the ground or your hands, but *don't*! Look through that turn and focus on where your bike is going to be three seconds from now. This is what will ultimately get you through the tight turn.

Safety First

Time to be real. Tight turns are not easy. What makes things even worse is they don't occur a lot in your average daily riding. The truth of the matter is, in order to do a locked or really tight turn, you are going to have to practice to the point that you can do it in your sleep. If you ride and practice a lot, the friction zone and associated fine-muscle control will become second nature to you. This is when you will accidentally do your first locked turn during practice. And once you get it once, it will start happening more and more. Then on the rare occasion you do have to make a really tight turn out on the road, you will be ready for it, and it will cause you no heartache whatsoever. But until you're ready for a tight turn, you have to remember the underlying and golden rule of motorcycle riding, the rule that governs everything: safety first.

Fortunately, a situation involving a tight turn is not just going to jump up and grab you. You know why? Because you plan ahead and always know what's coming up next. You'll be aware of any tight turn situation before you're knee-deep in it. But as you're approaching it, you have to be asking yourself: "Is this a turn I can do?" If you doubt your skill or the situation, don't risk it. Stop the bike in a straight line and attack the turn in whatever manner is within your skill set. Or turn as sharply as you can and stop when you have to, push the bike back a little bit, and finish the turn. Or, make sure traffic is clear and swing wide if room is available. You can power-walk it, or some of it, until you're sure you've got it under control, then finish the turn with your feet up. Don't let your pride get you in trouble. I want you to show me in the motorcycle rider's rule book where it says you can't stop along the side of the road before the turn and figure out a plan of attack that will work for you.

> "You cannot begin to imagine how much this simple step helps get you through that tight turn."

Turning from a stop in heavy moving traffic can be tricky and even dangerous—trying to coordinate fine-muscle control, getting the bike moving, stable, and turned while trying to hit a too-small target.

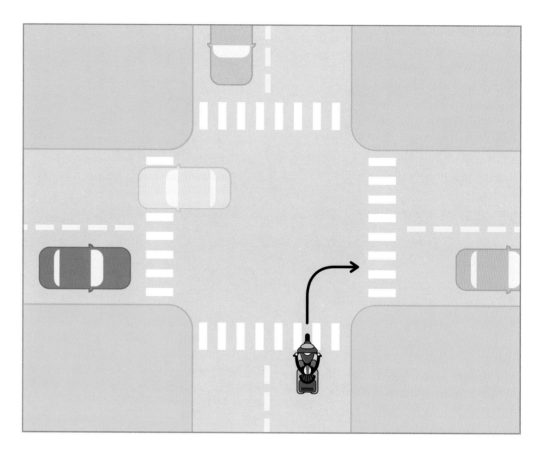

One last thing about tight turns, they may pop up because you didn't plan ahead well enough . . . or maybe you were daydreaming and blew right past your turn-in point. These are not roadway-designed tight turns, they are "Oops, I wasn't thinking" tight turns. Say, for example, you are riding along, enjoying the scenery, and you suddenly realize you need to turn just up ahead. You are able to get yourself slowed or stopped but not in time to make a nice, normal turn. Now you have to handle the tight turn you are faced with in whatever manner is safest for you.

And, once again, in slow, tight turns, what is the Golden Rule? *Stay away from that front brake lever.* Use the rear brake. When you have that motorcycle locked into a tight turn and you accidentally stop that front wheel, that big bike will want to fall over to its point of lowest potential. Front brake in tight turns = practice in picking up your big bike.

Turning from a Stop

There are a couple of different ways to turn from a stop: the moving turn and the curbside pullout. Each has its place in the real world. Imagine you're at an intersection controlled by a stoplight and you need to make a right turn. No big deal, except cross-traffic is really heavy. You can't sit there all day, holding up the folks behind you. You have to move. This problem is best solved with a moving turn. That is, get the motorcycle moving and balanced, then make your turn.

Or maybe you're at a shopping mall. You got a really good spot and got your bike pointed at an easy getaway—against the flow. But now there's an impatient blue-haired gal waiting for your spot. You're stuck now. Your easy "cheater" turn is gone. But if you make a tighter turn, with the flow, it's an open shot right on out of the parking lot to freedom. Here's where you need to know the curbside pullout.

Here you thought you could flout the rules a bit and scoot right out. But you forgot how valuable your front-row parking space is on a busy Saturday. Now you're faced with a tricky turn and very little room to pull it off.

Your practice "walking the line" in Chapter 2 will pay off here. Get the bike moving first, then coordinate your low-speed turn into traffic when your motorcycle's stable. Once you commit, don't look back. Focus on where you want the bike to be.

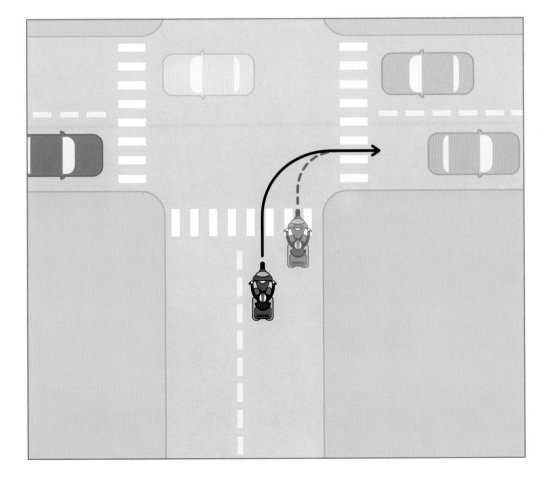

Riding Drill Number 3
CURBSIDE PULLOUT

Sharp turns from a stop are not difficult, but for maximum control they take lots and lots of practice. Fortunately, you don't need a lot of room to do them, and they're kinda fun.

Start out practicing the 90-degree pullout. Throw down some cones or use some existing lines in a parking lot to mark your boundaries. Use the friction zone to get the bike turned, then release the clutch and roll on the throttle when you know you've nailed it. When this starts to become comfy for you, in both directions, take it to the next level and work on the 135.

Going left (in North America) from a 135-degree angle is a lot easier than going right, obviously. But practice going both directions anyway. Practice this drill once a month for one full hour.

There is a way to practice this as part of your daily riding program. When you ride your big bike to the store and park, find a spot where you can pull all the way through into the next space so that you are pointed out of the space. When you go to leave the parking lot, make a sharp right-hand turn out of the space and focus on staying in the right half of the lane.

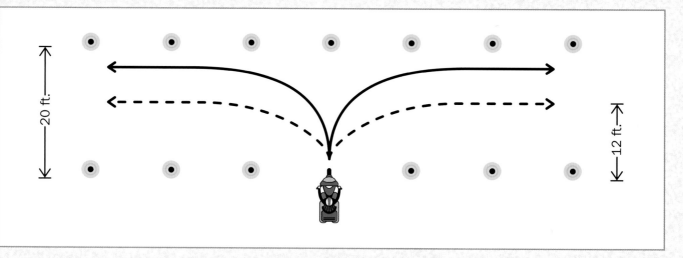

The 90-degree curbside pullout. Start with the cones spaced 20 feet apart, and work your way down to 12 feet. Begin the turn from a stop at the X. Practice in both directions until you can do it in one smooth motion, then start tightening up your turn in preparation for the real deal: the 135-degree curbside pullout.

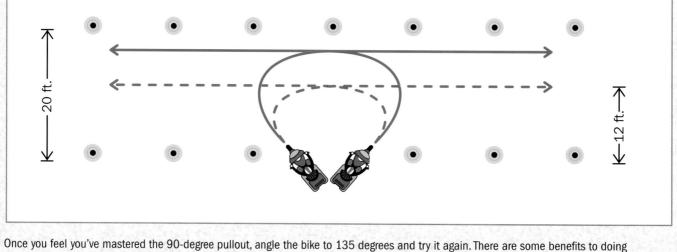

Once you feel you've mastered the 90-degree pullout, angle the bike to 135 degrees and try it again. There are some benefits to doing this, but mostly it's just good practice—and a lot of fun, requiring a lot of skill.

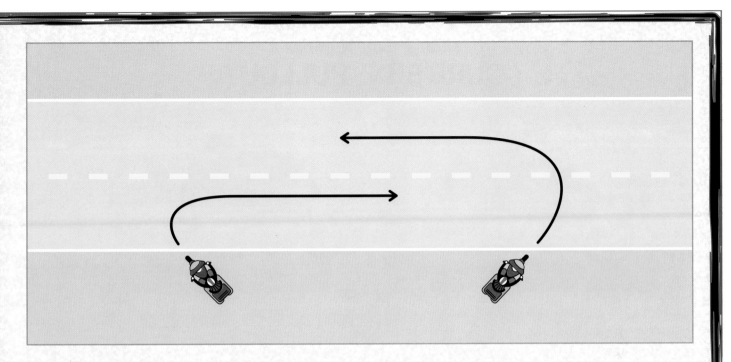

The 135-degree curbside pullout is an old motorcycle cop maneuver. Facing left makes it easier to nab speeders. For average riders, having a good view of the oncoming traffic (without craning your neck over backward) gives you a good safety advantage. When practicing this and performing it in the real world, do not attempt this maneuver with *any* traffic nearby until you feel completely comfortable turning into a 12-foot width—and even then, make sure traffic is clear.

Start with your inside foot planted, handlebars turned, bike slightly leaned over, and head and eyes directed into the turn.

Riding Drill Number 3
CURBSIDE PULLOUT

2

3

Smoothly ease the clutch into the friction zone while simultaneously opening the throttle.

Pick your foot up right away for better control and stability.

Once the bike is stable, lean it into the turn and get it pointed in the direction you intend to go.

4

5

6

Once you have the bike pointed in the right direction, smoothly release the clutch completely and open the throttle for acceleration.

Practice the 90-degree curbside pullout once a month for an hour until it's perfect every time. Once you've got the 90 nailed, start working on the 135.

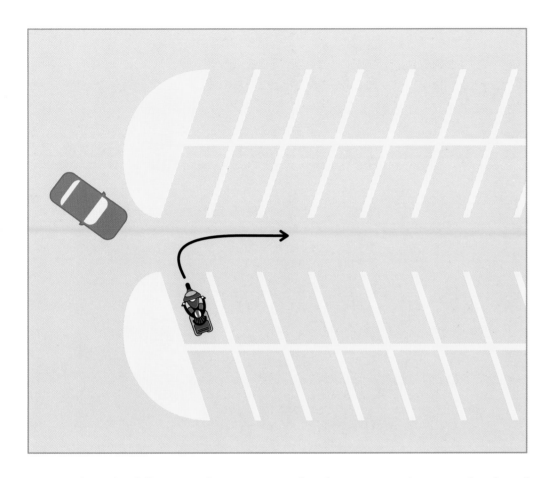

This move requires you to do everything at once: use the friction zone, turn the handlebars, balance, and look through the turn. Use Riding Drill Number 3 to practice this maneuver.

So what's the difference? They're both low-speed, right-hand turns. However, at the intersection, if you've planned ahead, you can leave yourself a little bit of straight-line room before your turn. This means that you can get moving and balanced before you have to make the sharp turn. In the parking spot, you've got no room to do this, so you have to start from a stop while turning.

At the intersection, you left yourself some room to get moving, so start out moving very slowly in a straight line, just like you practiced in Chapter 2. Find the sweet spot with the friction zone and throttle, and get your feet up on the pegs/boards. Time your approach to maximize the gap in traffic. Once you're committed, turn your head and eyes and focus on where you want to go—not at the oncoming traffic. This is good planning, confident decision-making, and low-speed riding skills at

their best. Nice work! Remember that, if during your turn, or right at the end of it, you have to slow or stop suddenly, use just the rear brake.

As for that shopping-mall parking space, it's time to go. No room to start out going straight, you've got to start with those handlebars turned. Everything at once now, the motorcycle is straight up and down, and your body is right over the top of your bike. Find that sweet spot in the friction zone and the throttle, then get comfy with your clutch hand stretched way out and your throttle hand tucked into your ribs. Look where you want to go, coordinate that fine-muscle control, and get that bike turned. Take a few baby steps to get started if you need to, but get those feet up as quick as you can. Hold those handlebars through that turn. Once you know you've made the turn, smoothly release the clutch as you roll on the throttle for a clean getaway.

Low-Speed Maneuvers Part Two

▮ **Counterweighting** ▮ **More U-Turns**
▮ **Parking**

After smooth, tight turns from a stop, it's time to venture into the world of U-turns. U-turns are like tight turns in many respects. They don't happen a lot, but they do happen way more often than tight turns, and they are the most hated turns in motorcycle land—especially big-bike land. One good thing about U-turns, they don't sneak up and bite you. You will always have some type of notice that you are going to have to make a U-turn before it happens. This alone lets you pre-plan your U-turn and, for the most part, pick the location where you want to make it.

Counterweighting

We have to be honest right up front: counterweighting is not a technique that we use in everyday riding very often. It's not something we see anybody else use much either. It's an advanced technique that comes in handy during police motor training and Shriner drills. That said, it's a technique that you should be comfortable with, and it will definitely help you with those slow, tight turns and U-turns when necessary.

Before you add counterweighting into your practice sessions, let us say this: it is important that you be completely comfortable with the friction zone and have your coordinated fine-muscle control adjustments down to habits you could perform in your sleep. Counterweighting is a technique best used in slow, controlled riding as an assist to balance while turning. And like everything else in the world of motorcycle skills, it requires lots of practice to get comfortable with it.

Counterweighting shifts your body weight to the outside while you are leaning the motorcycle way over into a turn. It's an exaggeration of the technique described earlier of keeping your body upright and over the motorcycle while leaning it at very slow speeds. This exaggerated

weight shift puts your weight slightly outside the motorcycle's center of mass, which helps offset a dramatic lean and provides a feeling of greater stability. (Roadracers do the same thing, only the opposite, to counteract high-speed turning forces and increase cornering clearance. This is referred to as "leaning in" or "hanging off," which we'll discuss in a later chapter.)

Put bluntly, counterweighting means weighting the outside peg and moving your butt over on your seat until the edge of your motorcycle seat is now in your "centerline" (sorry, but that's the nicest way we could think of to say that). Doing this adds to your feeling of stability and can reduce your turning radius, but beware—by definition, it reduces your cornering clearance.

Although we said at the beginning that we don't often use this technique, this doesn't mean you shouldn't try it! You never know when the additional skill will come in handy. But, as we said before, start out slow and be patient with yourself. Don't rush things.

U-Turns

In Chapter 3 we discussed how to practice figure eights. See, figure-eight practice gives you three things for the price of one. When you practice your figure eights, you are pretty much forcing yourself to practice the fiction zone. This is why we talked about doing figure eights after becoming familiar with the friction zone. But, isn't a figure eight just an extended right or left turn—or a U-turn? You bet it is. If you practice your figure eights to the point where you can do them locked, then you can for sure do a locked right or left turn or a U-turn. And they are really easy to practice. Whenever you get on the bike and head out on a ride, to go to work, or to go to the store, just make a great big figure eight along the way.

Opposite: Hanging off is an advanced technique used by professional riders and unabashed showoffs. It's rarely necessary in street riding, but if you want additional skills to hone and use, counterweighting can come in handy—and it looks kinda cool.

"... counterweighting means weighting the outside peg and moving your butt over on your seat until the edge of your motorcycle seat is now in your 'centerline'..."

Get your position set before you lean the bike and start the turn. Move over in the seat so the edge of the seat is splitting your butt in two. Put as much of your weight as possible on the outside peg or floorboard. Turn your head and look back over your shoulder to where your bike's going to be in about three seconds. Turn those handlebars and use the friction zone to keep your bike moving smoothly, all the way through the turn. Don't be surprised when you start scraping hard parts on the ground!

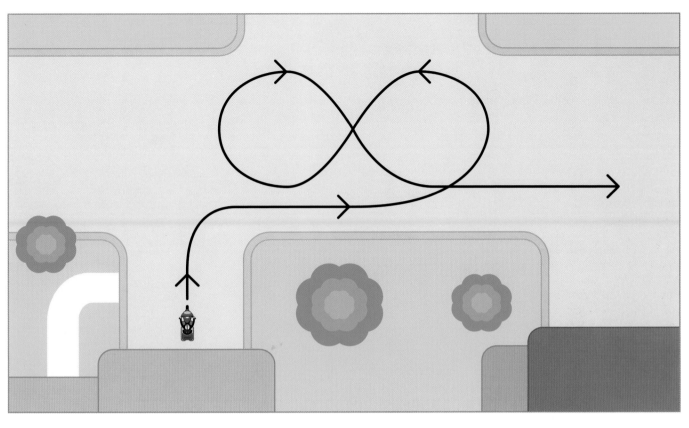

Give U-turns a whirl every time you leave your driveway and every time you come home.

Pull out of your driveway and start heading down your nice, quiet, residential street. When traffic's clear, slow or stop and make a U-turn to the left. Cross over to the wrong side of the street, then make a U-turn to the right. This takes all of about ten seconds, and you'll be heading back in your originally desired direction. And you just practiced turning, friction zone, and coordinated muscle control. Repeat this process every time you come home from riding your motorcycle.

Practice tip: every time you make a U-turn, make it as sharp as you comfortably can. Always try to finish your U-turn as close to the center of the roadway as you can. Once you are really comfortable with the tight U-turns, the wide ones are easy. But, if you want to know the truth, even though you can do the wide ones really easy, you will want to do as tight a U-turn as you safely can because it

makes you feel good about the control you have of your big bike.

U-turn secret: if you can comfortably make U-turns in both directions on the residential street in front of your house, then you will most likely be able to handle a U-turn at just about any intersection you will come across out on the road.

Sometimes you will get on some very narrow roadways out in the rural areas where you may ride. There may come a time where you will be forced to make a U-turn on one of these narrow roads that are simply too narrow for you to make a U-turn on. That is fine. Turn as much as you can, stop before going off the edge of the pavement, push the motorcycle backward however far you have to, and then finish up the U-turn.

The same thing can be said for gravel. At some point you may end up on a gravel road or in a gravel parking lot, and you are going to have to make

Riding Drill Number 4
IRON CROSS

Motor officers use a drill called the iron cross. Average riders can use an adapted version at any quiet intersection. Find a four-way stop with no traffic at the end of a long day. Carve out a path of travel that resembles a giant four-leaf clover—it'll be four tight turns interspersed with four U-turns. Of course, do it in both directions. You should spend 15 to 30 minutes twice a week performing this exercise.

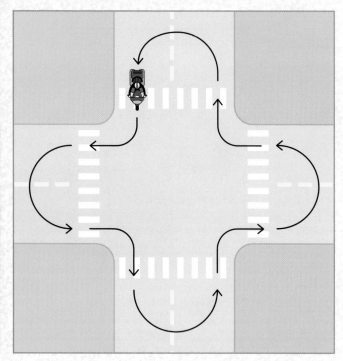

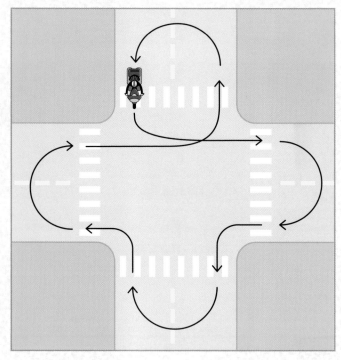

The adapted iron cross combines four sharp turns with four U-turns, alternating one after another. Practice this in both directions, two to three times each direction, twice a week, at the end of a ride.

Note that going left (in North America) means you'll be turning the "wrong way." Make absolutely sure there's no other traffic in sight, and stop after each circuit of the iron cross to reassess traffic. If necessary, only practice this drill when you can be sure traffic is nil, or mark out an iron cross in an empty parking lot instead.

1

2

Stay off of the front brake lever, and use your rear brake only; ride the rear brake if you are comfortable using that technique.

Find that sweet spot in the friction zone and with your throttle control.

3

Get those handlebars turned as sharply as you can.

4

Make fine-muscle control adjustments in the friction zone and throttle as needed.

5

Get that head turned and those eyes up. Look to where you want your motorcycle to go. No checking out the ground for money, it ain't there.

6

Hold those handlebars throughout your turn; don't let them bounce and make you pull them back in.

7

Stay in an upright position and over your motorcycle all of the way through the turn.

8

Use counterweighting if you're comfortable practicing that technique. However, with this many turns in this small of a space, counterweighting can be rather cumbersome . . . and it's really not necessary.

Don't be in a hurry to grab a spot as soon as you see it. Take your time, make a few sighting passes, and plan out your park job. Looping around, circling, and low-speed riding back and forth past the spot while you formulate your plan of attack is good low-speed practice anyway.

Quick: do you see the motorcycle in both of these photos? Position your motorcycle within a parking space in a manner that maximizes visibility.

a U-turn or maybe even a tight turn. Whatever turn you have to make under these conditions, you should do it in the safest, most comfortable way for you. Your safety and your comfort are your number one priorities whenever you are out riding and come across new or unusual conditions.

Parking

Man, how tough can this be? We do it all the time in our cars, right? Pull into the space, stop, get out, and go about your business. What more is there to know? A lot more. Riding a heavyweight motorcycle requires a little additional planning, and in the case of parking, poor planning can make your life a lot harder.

The first thing we have to acknowledge, obviously, is that cars can back up on their own. Most motorcycles can't. So remember, every time you nose that bike into a spot, you may have to push it backward to get it out. So, before you take any parking space, make sure you are going to be able to get your big bike out of the space you take.

On a two-wheel, single-track vehicle like a motorcycle, a sloping surface has both advantages and disadvantages. When parking, a little planning ahead can turn any slope into an advantage. The overarching rule of thumb with parking a big bike, or any bike, is to park with the bike pointed uphill whenever possible. Or, put another way, any time you know you're going to have to back your bike up, try to park so you'll be backing the bike downhill.

The second rule of parking—and this may come as a bit of a surprise—is to try to *enjoy* the process. Take your time and pick just the right spot, and plan out your angle of attack thoughtfully. Don't ever park your bike in a hurry just because you have somewhere to be. Scoping out the perfect parking spot and planning how

This rider was in too much of a hurry to get parked and has left himself in a real pickle, trying to get that big mother out of there. Always park with your back wheel into the curb, pointed uphill.

to use it, even if it means making several passes on the street or in a parking lot, is good low-speed maneuver practice anyway. Have fun with it. If you know you're going to have to back the bike in, this gives you an opportunity to wait to do it when traffic is a little lighter.

On the street, plan to put your back wheel close to or against the curb, with the front tire pointed out toward traffic. If the street's going uphill, you're golden, and you can angle your bike toward the flow of traffic for a clean getaway. If the street's going downhill, you should angle your bike against the flow of traffic and plan on making a sharp turn when you leave.

In a parking lot, again, take your time and enjoy the process. Whenever possible, find two open spots nose-to-nose and pull all the way through for a clear escape route. Making a sharp turn on your way out is more fun than having people watch you push it out backward.

There are a few other tips you should know for parking. Always, always use motorcycle-specific parking if it's available. It makes for a good show of rider solidarity, and it doesn't unnecessarily use up parking spots that are meant for cars. Avoid the urge to pull your bike right up onto a sidewalk or next to a building so it's "safer." Regardless of your reasoning, it mostly just pisses off the non-riding public. Put it in the lot like everybody else.

> **"Be careful with parking on hot asphalt, which can suck a sidestand down and leave you with a bike to pick up."**

The relatively cool temperature of the surface of the paint here can help prevent your sidestand from sinking into the asphalt.

Be careful with parking on hot asphalt, which can suck a sidestand down and leave you with a bike to pick up. If you know the surface is soft, find a painted line or concrete curb to set your sidestand on; the bike is less likely to sink that way. In a parking lot, don't pull all the way into a space. Leave the end of the bike even with the outside end of the spot. This makes your bike clearly visible to other drivers who might be in a bit of a rush and not see your bike tucked in there. If they pull in too quickly, they're liable to knock your bike over . . . and then leave.

And then there's parking your bike at motorcycle events and rallies. Rarely is there ever a rhyme or reason to the parking structure; folks just park where it's convenient, and usually close together. This can create challenges for anyone who isn't a full-time motor officer. The same principles still apply, though. Park facing uphill and take your time to select your spot. And don't hesitate to walk your bike into your parking spot if you have to. There is absolutely no shame in pushing your bike into a tight place rather than risking a mistake that sends a whole row of bikes toppling over!

One last thing: we've mentioned more than once that you should take your time when you perform low-speed maneuvers. This is true in all things motorcycle-related. Don't ever hurry on a motorcycle, ever. If you're in a hurry, take the car. Hurrying puts the destination before the ride, which is opposite of what we want to do on a motorcycle. Ride fast if you want to, but don't ever, ever be in a hurry.

Basic Braking

▌ **The Braking Spectrum**
▌ **Weight Transfer** ▌ **Basic Braking Smoothness**

Busted myth number one: At the tires, there is little difference between a big bike and a little bike when it comes to braking. Sure, the bigger bike is heavier, so its tires and braking components are designed to handle the extra load. Side by side, in the hands of riders with similar abilities, a stock dresser and a stock sportbike will stop in about the same distance.

Previous page: Your brakes are the most powerful tools in your arsenal. Use them wisely. *Yamaha Motor Corp.*

Braking doesn't seem very complicated to most riders. You use the brakes to stop the bike, right? Grab the lever or push the pedal, right? Wrong. There's more to it than that. Arguably the most important skill for maximum control is the ability to bring the bike to a smooth, safe stop—no matter what else may be going on. Stopping your big bike, and using your brakes for maximum effectiveness, is a must-have skill in every rider's arsenal.

Think of your brakes as a tool you use to apply pressure. A screwdriver is a good example. If you use too light a touch, not only will you not be able to turn the screw, but you'll probably strip out the head too, leaving you with an additional problem to solve. Too heavy a hand can quickly go wrong as well, sending the screwdriver skittering sideways across perfect paint or chrome, leaving an ugly scar.

The same approach applies to braking: for some purposes, you need a lot of pressure, for others, only a little—and each time is a little different. Knowing when to apply the pressure, how much pressure to apply, and where and how exactly to apply it are skills that separate the pros from the amateurs. Don't fear, you are already on your way to becoming a pro. You already drive a car too, right? Well, the situations you face on the road while driving your car are the same as those you will face on your motorcycle. This means you already have the basic knowledge you need for braking in different situations. Now, all you have to do is work on getting your braking habits down pat on your motorcycle.

How Is Braking a Big Bike Different?

So, the question you're probably asking is this: what is the difference between braking a big bike and a little bike? Or, for that matter, what is the difference between braking a Volkswagen Bug and braking a big SUV? Take a moment to stop and think about both questions.

At the wheels, there's almost no difference between braking a big bike and a little bike. The braking components' design and size are meant to achieve the same result—slow the bike efficiently and effectively. Big bikes can stop just as quickly—sometimes even more quickly—than the hottest street-legal sportbike. The biggest difference in braking is in what you *feel*: in the seat of your pants, in the tips of

The best way to hone your braking skills is just to get out there and rack up the miles. While you do so, you have to practice consciously and deliberately the perfect braking technique for every slowdown, every stop, every time. Repetition of the bare-bones basics is the first key to success. *American Honda Motor Co.*

your fingers, in your palms, in your butt, and in your toes.

No matter what actual differences may or may not exist between little bikes and big bikes, what is important is your *interpretation of* and *reaction to* the differences. Physically, there will be lots of differences, such as the positioning of your feet, the difference in feedback from footpegs to floorboards, and the wider bike and seat, which will give you a different seating position and a different view from the rider's seat. All of these things are going to have an effect on how the bike feels, and what it feels like it's doing, in a riding situation like braking.

Of course, the most obvious difference is that the added weight of the bike makes low-speed riding more precarious. We learned that in the last few chapters. If you stop your bike with the slightest bit of lean to one side or another, or stop it slightly too early, before you've squared up, you have to balance quite a bit of weight with your legs to keep the machine from falling over. So your braking has to be well planned and very smooth.

The differences between a big bike and a smaller bike are also going to be unique to each rider because every rider has a different understanding of how a bike works, a different riding style, a different approach to solving problems—and every bike is geometrically and ergonomically different.

But no matter what the bike feels like, the most important thing is that the feeling and feedback have to become your new "normal" feeling. You have to make it your own. You have to get intimately familiar with how your big bike brakes for you and how it reacts to braking in various situations and with varying amounts of pressure. The only way to do this is to get out and ride that bike, put in the time and put on the miles, and actively practice your

braking all the time, because braking is a life-saving skill. And the best way to keep it sharp is to make it and keep it second nature.

The Braking Spectrum

There are gradations to braking, both rider-based and situation-based. On the rider-based side, there are those who are too tentative and afraid to actually use the brakes because they fear throwing the bike into a skid or going over the handlebars. On the other end, you've got riders with hams for fists who use the brakes like an on/off switch, a technique that is only marginally effective . . . though great fun to watch from the sidelines. Maximum braking control means you can sense correctly what is needed, and your hands and feet know how to apply exactly the inputs required for any given situation. In order to do this, you have to be completely comfortable with your big bike every moment you ride. You have to trust your tires, trust your bike, and trust yourself.

On the road, different riding situations require different braking solutions, and these cover a wide spectrum as well. There are the slight, subtle adjustments necessary to set the perfect entry speed to a corner. There are the run-of-the-mill smooth stops at a stoplight or stop sign. There are the midrange braking maneuvers, such as bringing the bike down from 70 to 40 miles per hour for an exit ramp—or suddenly slowing for a car moving at 40 miles per hour merging into 70-mile-per-hour traffic. And there are the extreme situations in which you need to use both brakes to their maximum potential to avoid becoming a hood ornament on a Mack truck. So maximum braking control also means knowing how much braking is needed in a given situation.

> **"Maximum braking control means you can sense correctly what is needed, and your hands and feet know how to apply exactly the inputs required for any given situation."**

The second key to success: setting aside dedicated practice time. After riding home from work, swing through the nearest empty parking lot and practice your quick stops for a few minutes. After a long Saturday ride out in the country, spend the last 10 to 20 minutes of your day flexing those braking muscles.

As a rider there is always a chance that you will be tested by having to use maximum possible braking at one time or another—whether you've had lots of practice or not. Under unusual and extreme conditions it is very, very difficult to be perfect, and even under normal conditions, it is rare to always get it exactly right. Errors just naturally creep in; after all, you are only human. Because you are only human, the more you have to think about what you are doing, the greater your chance of making an error. And, if you stop to think about what you have to do, you waste precious braking time. So your goal is to be as up to date with your skills as possible, to make sure your skills are also your habits, and then you hope that being able to do it 99 percent correctly is enough.

So what does it take to get good at braking? It is only through repetition—lots and lots of miles, and lots and lots of deliberate practice—that you can control both the front and rear brakes to their greatest potential. You have to put in the time and let your body memorize how the bike feels in different situations and how the motorcycle responds to different rider inputs. You have to make effective braking a habit, something that happens in every situation without ever having to think about it. You also want

Even though the amount of braking action required changes depending on each particular situation, the actual braking techniques themselves don't change. Understand the techniques, and you can apply them to every situation, in varying degrees, to maintain maximum control of your bike.

On both four- and two-wheeled vehicles, the brake pedal is meant to be pressed with the ball of your foot. In a four-wheeler, that means it's your thigh—one of the biggest, most imprecise muscles on your body—that stops the car. A motorcycle's rear brake is much more sensitive than that and relies on the use of the lower leg and the ankle to pivot the foot for a more precise braking pressure. It's another example of the fine-muscle control needed to ride smoothly.

your overall technique to be the same thing every time: both brakes, front and rear, every time, no matter what.

Effective braking can save your life, so build those skills right and build them strong. Fortunately, maximum braking control is relatively straightforward. Remember, a bike is just a machine that will do exactly what you tell it to do—if you've learned how to speak its language.

Basic Braking Smoothness

As you've probably guessed already, good braking is all about getting into the habit. You have to develop and set in stone the technique of smooth, steady, increasing pressure on both brakes, as opposed to grabbing, stomping, jabbing, pulling, and jerking your way to a stop. That sounds easy enough, and in reality, it is. Every stop, every time, use your right hand and right foot to apply smooth and steady, increasing pressure on that brake lever and brake pedal.

As for the pedal that's situated at your right foot, you already have lots of practice using that. Most of us drive a car or light truck, at least on a semi-regular basis, so we've already got the rear brake down pat. Or so we would think. Here is the rub: unlike on a car, that bike's foot pedal only controls one wheel instead of four (ignoring for now linked and integrated braking systems.) And the stopping power of the actual brake components at your big bike's wheel is comparable to the power your car has available to *all four* of its wheels. This can pose a problem to the unwary rider.

When you slow or stop your car, you use just one pedal, and one pressure input goes to all four wheels. But on your bike you have two separate systems, front and rear, so you squeeze the front and press the rear, applying a constant amount of pressure. Here's the problem: when you start to brake, you begin to transfer weight toward the front of the bike. This means the back of the bike is carrying less weight, so it doesn't need quite as much pressure to do its job as the front of the bike does. It also means the front of the bike needs more pressure to do its job properly. So here's lesson number one: train yourself to use less pressure with your right foot and more pressure with your right hand, all the while applying smooth, steady, increasing pressure to both. Once again, this is a case of highly developed, coordinated fine-muscle control.

It's really easy for your brain to say, "Hey. Pressure time. Right hand, you squeeze. Right foot, you press," and allow the control inputs to end there. The right hand and right foot have their commands, so they start doing their thing—and the next thing you

No matter what your upright, in-control, big bike is doing, gravity pulls the bike more or less straight down through the center of mass. Note that under normal riding circumstances, the center of mass is just ahead of the center of the bike, so if you need to brake, the front wheel will need to do more work than the rear wheel. This is why you need more pressure on the front brake than on the rear brake.

Acceleration causes a shift in the center of mass of the motorcycle. The rear wheel is doing all of the work to move the big bike forward, so there is a weight shift rearward, which moves the center of mass rearward. The rearward weight shift also causes a compression of the rear suspension, which lowers the overall height of the bike. This, in turn, also lowers the center of mass.

know, you've used too much pressure on the rear brake and locked it up. (This creates a new set of problems all its own, which we will discuss later.) When you are riding your big bike, you have to teach the brain to say instead,

"Hey. Pressure time. Right hand, you squeeze. Right foot, you press . . . but not as hard as the hand is squeezing." You have to build good habits from the very beginning and use them precisely,

When braking, there is a forward weight shift, the amount of which depends on how hard the braking is. The forward weight shift moves the big bike's center of mass forward and compresses the front suspension, lowering the overall height of the bike, which lowers the center of mass also.

Under heavy braking, the bike's mass shifts even more forward, causing even more front suspension compression. Once again, to correspond with the weight shift and height of the bike, the center of mass moves forward and down. This gives you the sensation of loading up the front tire. Don't sweat it. Continue to squeeze the front brake progressively harder, as if you're squeezing the juice out of an orange, while pressing the rear brake with less pressure. Note that in heavy braking, the front wheel is doing easily three quarters of the work to stop your big bike. This is why developing good braking habits through lots of practice is so important.

even in the most ordinary of situations, because you use the same habits in a low-stress environment as you do in an emergency. Use both brakes, smooth and steady, with increasing pressure, a little more on the front and a little less on the rear, every stop, every time.

Making the Most of the Rear Brake

In the Friction Zone section we mentioned feathering and riding the rear brake to add another degree of low-speed control. The key to getting the fine-muscle control on that rear brake is to keep that right foot in contact with the floorboard or footpeg, whichever your bike might have. The back half of your foot (the heel for floorboards, and the arch or heel for pegs) stays in contact with the board or peg.

Let's go back to braking your car. In your car you just move your foot from the gas pedal to the brake, simple enough. However, to move that foot from gas to brake you use your whole leg! You actually use your upper leg to pick up your lower leg, with the foot attached, and move it to the brake. Then, you use your lower leg to control your foot and upper leg to apply pressure to your car's brake pedal. Not a whole lot of fine-muscle control going on here—and way too much muscle for your motorcycle foot brake.

For the rear brake pedal on your motorcycle, the muscles that control your foot are all that you need. And the way you isolate those muscles so that you don't get that upper leg muscle involved? Keep your foot in contact with the floorboard or peg.

As you are riding along, place your right foot so that the ball of your foot, the part just behind the toes, is resting next to the brake pedal on the outside. Now, when it comes time to brake, all you have to do is *pivot* the front of your foot up (keeping the back in contact with the board or peg), rotate it slightly

While it may be that cornering skill is most important here, your success relies on setting a good entry speed for the corner. Being able to modulate (adjust) your braking to achieve the exact speed you want at the exact moment you want is a very subtle skill.

to the left, and press on the brake pedal. Note that on bikes with stretched-out forward controls and a long reach to the brake pedal, this technique becomes difficult at best.

This requires minimal motion and effort over a short distance, and now your foot is where it needs to be to apply smooth and steady, precise, increasing pressure for whatever the situation demands. You have the fine-muscle control that you need to apply that rear brake in the most effective manner.

Braking to Slow

Normal braking situations are nothing new for you. They're the same situations you see when you're driving your car. For example, you are coming up to a line of cars stopped at a red light, and since you have good visual habits, your eyes are up and looking well ahead. You see the light has changed to green. You know the distance between you and the back of the line is large enough that you are not going to have to stop, you're just going to slow down a bit to let the line start moving before you get there.

Another example is riding along a country road and slowing down to make a 90-degree right turn at the next intersection. Or maybe you are out doing what most motorcycle riders live for: searching out and carving up all the twisty roads you can find. For both of these situations, you need to set a safe and appropriate entry speed for the turn.

So how do we do this? Just like we would when driving our cars, except the actual mechanics are a little different.

One really quick note—as you sit here and read about the process of braking, it may have the feeling of being separate steps or actions in time: brake, look, adjust, look again, brake some more, look some more, and so on. But it is not! This is one continuous, smooth, flowing action from start to finish. Although we read it one step at a time, in the real world, the transitions are ideally seamless.

The right hand provides smooth, steady, increasing pressure, squeezing the front brake lever, using a little more pressure than on the rear brake pedal. This happens while the right foot provides smooth, steady, increasing pressure, pressing the rear brake pedal, using a little less pressure than on the front brake lever. The rear of your right foot is on the peg or board, the ball of your right foot is on the brake pedal, and you are using the muscles in your foot on the brake pedal.

You start out with light pressure at first, to get the braking action started and slow the motorcycle just a bit. Your head and eyes are still up, and you are evaluating the situation, your speed, and your position.

The constant adjusting of the brakes in order to get your slowing just right is also called modulation. So let's modulate using this situation: coming up behind a line of cars just as the light turns green. Say your hand is applying 10 pounds per square inch (psi) of pressure at the front brake lever and your foot is applying 7 psi to the rear brake pedal. (These are just made-up numbers. They could be 5 and 3.5, or 20 and 14, or 100 and 70. It's the relative difference and the modulation to these numbers that's important to us.) You realize that you're closing too fast on the line of cars and you're going to have to stop before they all get moving. But you don't want to stop—the light's green. All you have to do is change your timing and/or rate of deceleration. So you modulate your braking to slow just a little quicker and just a little earlier in the maneuver, say, by increasing your front brake pressure to 11 psi and your rear brake pressure to 8 psi, then backing off again to 10 and 7 to time your arrival at the end of the line. It's nothing that anyone but you would notice—especially if you're smooth about it—and it buys you the extra time and space you need to avoid coming to a complete stop.

In addition to braking you will probably have to do some downshifting to match your gear to your forward speed. When the time is right for the situation you are in—traffic, right-hand turn, twisties, whatever the case may be—you smoothly ease off the brakes and continue on your way.

Smooth, precise modulation takes years of practice and many thousands of miles. Newbies often modulate 25 to 50 percent (from 10.0 psi to 12.5 or 15.0 psi) when they're learning, whereas experts may be able to modulate their inputs by as little as 5 to 10 percent (from 10.0 psi to 10.5 or 11.0 psi). At the controls, the difference between 10.0 and 11.0 psi might be a finger movement as small as 1/32 of an inch! Being able to measure out that sort of modulation requires a lot of time in the saddle.

To summarize, slowing and setting entry speed requires smooth, steady braking with increasing pressure on both brakes, adjusting and modulating as needed. Use less pressure on the rear brake pedal than on the front brake lever. This is how you slow your big bike, from start to finish, every trip and every time.

Braking to Stop

Once again, just because you are on a motorcycle doesn't mean that stopping situations are any different from those

Expert modulation of the brakes means making adjustments that probably can't be seen with the naked eye. Think of it as slightly varying amounts of pressure instead.

you face driving your car. It's just the mechanics of stopping that change. Just like braking to slow, use smooth, steady braking with increasing pressure on both brakes. Use less pressure on the rear brake pedal than on the front brake lever. That front brake is doing most of the work. To bring the bike to a smooth stop, you are going to continue your smooth brake application with your right hand and your right foot, judging the distance and closing speed to the exact point you want to stop and adjusting and modulating as necessary.

While you are doing this, downshift your bike all the way down to first gear. Do this as you slow, using the same shift points you would while accelerating. Whether you release the clutch or not after every gear change is up to you. Some riders do, others don't. It really doesn't matter. Either way, by the time you've stopped, your bike is already in first gear and ready to go. Remember this, if you do decide to release the clutch after every shift, you have just added engine braking into your wheel braking mix. In order to maintain your smooth, steady and precise braking, your adjusting and modulating skills

Many riders will argue the virtues of releasing the clutch after every downshift at a stop, or keeping the clutch squeezed the whole time as you shift down through the gears. The reality is that it doesn't matter which technique you use, as long as you're always in the right gear for the speed.

become more important. Now you are going to have to adjust and modulate the braking pressure with your right hand and right foot to take into account the slowing help of the engine.

Let's use the last example of coming up behind a line of cars at a stoplight, only this time, the light is still red. You don't have the choice just to slow down. So you've picked the spot where you want to stop, you are judging the amount of pressure your right hand and right foot are applying so that you can hit that spot precisely, and everything is going great. About 10 feet before your spot, your bike has slowed down exactly as you planned, and you know you'll hit your mark—but you also want to get your feet down quick to keep the bike from tipping over. So you take your right foot off of the brake and move both feet toward the ground to take a couple of steps as your big bike comes to a stop. Sorry! Wrong move. Try again.

Every time your foot is near the ground while that big bike of yours is moving forward, you run the risk of hurting yourself in a number of different ways. Your boot might find some gravel and you would have no traction. Or, just the opposite, you hit a soft spot or some debris and your foot sticks. Either of these scenarios can result in screwing up your knee in one way or another. Or maybe you are moving a little faster than you realized, and when your foot touches the asphalt it kicks back up behind you. If you're caught by surprise, you can lose your balance or destabilize the bike. If you have bags or crash bars, you can get your foot or lower leg kicked back into them. If you're lucky, this is just an embarrassing foot-down, scraped-boot moment. If you're unlucky, you could be facing a sprained or even broken ankle. On top of this, you also just lost your balance on your motorcycle, which is not a good thing if you just busted your ankle—try holding

Stick your feet out like a dirtbike or supermoto rider if you absolutely have to, but beware on a big bike. They're really not going to be able to help if something goes wrong. Best to keep your feet on the pegs or boards for better balance of the bike at slow speeds.

up an 800-pound bike on a broken bone! And, to make matters worse, you are no longer using smooth, steady pressure on both brakes. You took your right foot off of the brake pedal to put it down on the ground. You just willingly sacrificed half your technique and half your control. Balance and control are much improved with both feet on the pegs.

For maximum stopping control, you have to have your knees tight against the tank, your feet firmly on the pegs or floorboards, and that smooth pressure on both brakes until the bike comes to a complete stop. This helps keep the motorcycle stable and predictable as you get into that low-speed, low-stability territory under 15 miles per hour. The added weight of a big bike can bite you hard if your balance is anything less

than perfect: straight up and down, handlebars square.

Make no mistake about this: low speed is low speed. Your big bike does not care if it is stopping or riding in the friction zone, all it knows is that it is moving forward at a low speed. As was discussed in the friction zone chapters, at low speeds your best control of the bike comes from using the rear brake, not the front. Let us be a little bit more specific, in a stopping situation you have the most control by using the front brake in conjunction with the rear brake. If you take your right foot away from that rear brake pedal too soon and something happens at the very end where you need a little more stopping power, now all of that extra needed stopping power has to come from the

Riding along with your feet hovering over the ground as you stop may help you psychologically, but it doesn't do anything for your braking skills, balance, or smoothness. Your feet are not going to be much help on a moving bike if it suddenly wants to tip over. Better to use them to keep the bike balanced. Keep your feet on the pegs until the very last moment, just before or at the actual stop, when you can no longer keep the bike upright by balancing and need to plant your foot. Removing a foot too early upsets the bike's balance, reduces braking effectiveness in some cases, and can get you hurt if something goes wrong.

front brake; you are just asking for more practice in picking your big bike out of the middle of the street.

Keep that stopping pressure on both brakes, time it, modulate it, wait for it, and just before your big bike comes to a complete stop set your left foot—that is, your *left* foot—onto the ground first. Plant it at the exact moment your bike comes to a stop. Remember, that left foot is done shifting because you have

already down-shifted into first gear. Now it's on the ground, controlling the balance of your big bike, no steps, no chance of injury. And once your bike is stopped, you can take your right foot from the brake pedal and put it down on the ground to help with balance, if need be. In an ideal, perfectly balanced stop, you will have released the pressure on both brakes at the exact instant your bike comes to a complete stop. When

5 MPH

0 MPH

you do this right, you'll almost feel like you're hovering there on your bike, suspended in time and space. Neat.

So there we are again: a smooth, steady, increasing pressure on the brakes, more on the front, less on the rear, adjusting and modulating along the way, gliding to a perfect, balanced stop on your big bike. The left foot is down and planted just as the bike comes to a complete stop. After the stop the right foot can come down to help with the balance. The bike's in first gear and ready to go. Stop like this every trip, every time.

Are you starting to see a pattern here with braking techniques? Good. And think about it from a personal standpoint: if you only get this right one out of five times, well then, you know what you need to start practicing! It will come in handy as we move into more dramatic maneuvers.

Chapter 7

Emergency Braking

■ **Emergency Braking** ■ **Friction**
■ **Skidding**

It is far less likely on the road that you'll have to come to a complete stop in a braking situation. More often than not, situations only require you to slow down to buy yourself time and space. Being able to safely scrub off a lot of speed—rather than scrubbing it all off—is the most important braking skill you can have.

"**I** was out ridin' and this car pulls out in front of me. I had to lay 'er down."

I have heard this statement uttered so many times, and I can't think of a more ridiculous thing for a motorcyclist to say. What people mean when they say this is, "I don't know how to control my bike, so I locked up the rear brake and crashed on purpose."

But, what is actually true is this: "This car pulls out in front of me. I had no warning, no time, and no room to stop. And since I don't know how to use my brakes, I accidentally locked them up and crashed. And because it was really the other guy's fault, I refuse to take responsibility for it, so I'm going to pretend that I did it on purpose. No one will ever have to know that I don't know how to use my brakes."

These people are fooling themselves. They do not, and probably never will, understand that there is something more they need to learn about riding. They'll spend the rest of their lives blaming some dumb driver for forcing them to crash. And the worst part of all of this is that if the same situation happens again, they are going to do the exact same thing again, and they are going to go down again. The big question is will they be as lucky this time as they were last time?

Crashing on purpose is *not* an option to any semi-intelligent rider. The bike will stop a lot quicker with its rubber on the ground, rather than

Opposite: Many times when you see someone "lay it down," that person never even hit the car he or she was trying to avoid. Riders who know how to use their brakes can slow down or stop their bikes without crashing and then continue on their way. This rider has made a bad decision but will forever be blaming someone else for the mistake.

You might have to come to a complete stop for something like this, but more likely you'll only need to reduce speed quickly to keep a safe space cushion between you and the other driver. Don't try to use engine braking to assist in an emergency stop because it only increases the chance of a rear-wheel skid.

sliding along on its side. Throwing a bike to the ground in anticipation of a crash is the same as forfeiting a game because you're short one player. Do you want to give up without even *trying*?

Riders with maximum control can use both brakes to slow the bike dramatically and buy themselves time, or they can simply get the bike stopped to let the hazard clear out so they can continue on their way. If you don't know how to use your brakes, there's an easy solution (we have given you the information you need to learn how to develop good braking habits and skills), but don't fall into the trap of blaming another motorist when your skills—if you had learned and practiced them—could have prevented a crash.

Emergency Braking to Slow

Using heavy braking to slow down quickly—but not necessarily stop—is the single most important riding skill to have in your toolbox. It's the skill you'll have to use most often to avoid bad situations. Having to scrub off 30 to 60 miles per hour in just a few seconds is not uncommon in street riding. And in this author's experience, only rarely does an emergency situation require that you actually come to a complete stop. Most of the time all you need to do is slow, then go. And in a sudden-braking situation, you don't want to hang around too long anyway. A complete stop can make you a sitting duck as other vehicles come screeching up behind you.

Sometimes these situations sneak up on us, usually because we're not paying complete attention, and they'll require some emergency braking to get the motorcycle slowed down to a safer speed.

So what happens when you have to slow quickly for a car that pulled out in front of you? Or slow quickly from supra-legal freeway speeds to a suitable and sensible off-ramp speed? Or because someone else is trying to merge into 80-mile-an-hour traffic at ramp speed? It's broken-record time: the situations where you need to scrub off a lot of speed in a short amount of time are going to be the same on your motorcycle as they are in your car. There's nothing new here.

And guess what? The mechanics for doing this on your motorcycle are the same as those we discussed in the last chapter, with only a few tweaks. Right hand: squeeze brake lever with increasing pressure. Right foot: press brake pedal with increasing pressure. Modulate and adjust as needed. Downshift as needed. The increasing pressure on the front brake is greater than the increasing pressure on the rear.

And now, because it's heavy braking, you're increasing the pressure at a faster rate than you would in a normal setting. And let's remember that the rear brake pedal has only one tire to stop and not four, so don't let your car-driving

Riding Drill Number 5
SLOW AND GO

The key to good braking is to build good, consistent habits from the beginning. You've done this already by riding and practicing the same braking procedures for every stop. The benefit to having proper ingrained habits is that then it doesn't matter what the circumstances are. A normal, non-dramatic braking maneuver uses the same basic techniques as a drop-dead emergency.

So for this drill, start off slow and build yourself up to greater speeds. You'll need a fairly long stretch of asphalt, at least 300 feet. Identify a mark at 150 feet, or halfway, where you'll initiate your braking. Leave a landmark, such as a big stuffed animal or sack of potatoes, at your brake marker. Walk off increments of 25 feet (about an easy 10 steps) on either side of your brake marker and leave a different landmark at each one, from 75 feet all the way through 225 feet. Landmarks should all be unique and eye-catching to help you remember and compare your performance.

Continue to repeat the process, braking a little harder and slowing more on each pass, and noting your improvement. Evaluate yourself and be your own worst critic. Make sure that you did everything you had to do: proper braking technique each and every time, good control each and every time, head and eyes up each and every time. Also note if any improvement comes at a cost of being smooth and using consistent technique. If it does, back off a little bit and perfect smoothness and technique first, then work on braking performance.

Once down and back is one lap. Try to do at least 8 to 12 laps in a row, then take a short break and think about what you just did. Once you're comfortable with 25 miles per hour, bump it up to 30 to 35 miles per hour in fourth gear. From 35 miles per hour, try to get down to 10 miles per hour in less than 60 feet. You should practice this drill once a month for at least one full hour.

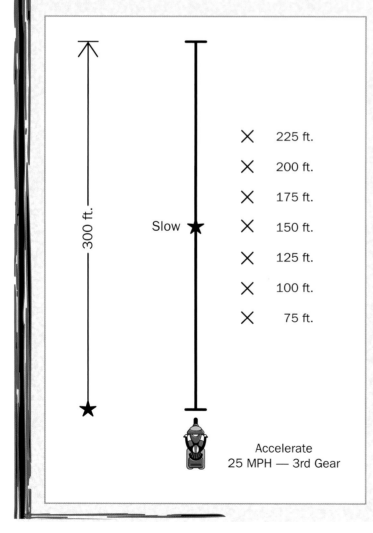

300 ft.

✕ 225 ft.

✕ 200 ft.

✕ 175 ft.

Slow ★ ✕ 150 ft.

✕ 125 ft.

✕ 100 ft.

✕ 75 ft.

Accelerate
25 MPH — 3rd Gear

1

Start from one end and accelerate up to about 25 miles per hour in third gear.

2

At your halfway mark, apply your brakes. The first few times through, to get the feel of everything, take it relatively easy and make sure that you are using the proper braking technique as described in the last chapter. Be certain to downshift as you brake. Once you think you have all the pieces in place, start braking harder and harder, making every effort to be smooth and in control at all times.

3

Your head and eyes should be up, looking forward. Do not worry about your speed, and don't stare down at your speedometer. When it feels like you have slowed to about 10 miles per hour, smoothly release the brakes and continue on your path at 10 miles per hour. Use your landmarks to make a mental note of how much room you needed to get from 25 to 10 miles per hour. You'll need to remember where you ended up so you can compare your braking performance to that of previous runs.

4

At the end of the line, make a U-turn and repeat the process in the opposite direction. Nothing says you can't practice two things at once, but make your braking skills your priority for this drill.

habits creep in. Since this is an urgent slowing situation, you need to make absolutely sure that you are applying less pressure on the rear brake pedal than you would in a car. This comes from constant repetition and everyday practice of the same basic motorcycle braking technique. Remember how we do this? For the front brake, squeeze with increasing pressure, kind of like squeezing the juice out of an orange. For the rear brake, *keep that heel on the floorboard or peg* and provide a little torque through the muscles of your ankle rather than pressure through the muscles of your leg. No surprises there, either.

As in any braking situation, visual skills are important, but they're particularly important in emergency situations. Your head and eyes are up, looking well ahead. You are focused in the direction of whatever it is that's requiring you to slow down, but you also have to be careful not to fixate on it. Keep scanning around to see what else might be going on and to find an escape route too. Make sure you're always in a gear that's consistent with your speed so you can instantly accelerate if the situation calls for it. Observe and decide whether you are slowing quickly enough, and modulate and adjust as necessary to be sure you're not going to run out of room. You're approaching the situation at the speed you've chosen and in the position and gear you've chosen, keeping an eye on closing distances and, in your head, timing everything, waiting for the "green light." Once all possible conflicts have been dealt with, smoothly release the brakes and proceed along your way.

So, are the reasons for always using the same braking trend or pattern starting to come into focus here? Good. Ordinary, everyday braking and stopping skills transfer seamlessly to heavy braking and emergency stopping techniques. All that's required, really, is

> "Make sure you're always in a gear that's consistent with your speed so you can instantly accelerate if the situation calls for it."

a little modulation and adjustment to the braking pressure.

Advanced High-Speed Method

You can practice scrubbing 15 to 25 miles per hour off your speed all you want to get a feel for the technique, but in the real world we're often going a lot faster than that. Unfortunately, there's rarely a good, safe place to practice this at high speeds except for a closed course like a track day. But when conditions are clear, you can take this emergency slowing technique to a much higher level.

Example: find a time when freeway traffic is light. Let yourself get into a position where there is no one behind you for at least a half a mile and there's no one who's going to interfere with you from an on-ramp. Cruise along at maximum highway speed, preferably 55 to 65 miles per hour, as you approach an interchange. When you get just past the point you might otherwise label "the point of no return," smoothly bring your bike down from 65 to about 25 miles per hour as quickly as you can, "pretending" that you actually want to try to make the exit. See if you can get your speed down to what would otherwise be a safe entry speed for the cloverleaf, done at the last minute.

When you feel like you've got the braking nailed down, another option is to toss in a lane change (from center to right lane), before you begin your braking, to make it even more realistic. If you try this, make *absolutely* certain you've finished the lane change and are riding in a straight line before you begin braking (see Chapter 10).

Like we said, the best place to perfect this advanced method is on a racetrack. Track days and training are not just for sportbike riders and racers! Having a closed-off circuit with lots of room, unlimited speed, and instructors

In this situation, as long as the road is otherwise empty, you have plenty of run-out room in case you make a mistake. If you feel unstable or suddenly lock one of the wheels, you can always abort the exercise, get the bike stable again, and try again at the next interchange.

close by can bring any rider up to the next level of control. And if you can ride in perfect comfort hauling your bike down from 120 to 30 miles per hour to make a sharp turn, you'll be ready for anything the street can throw at you.

Emergency Braking to Stop

Well, I hate to break with tradition here, so I won't. The approach to emergency stops is not much different from any other kind of braking maneuver.

First, emergency braking to a stop is just like emergency slowing, only now you are committed to stopping your motorcycle completely. Second, the emergency situations you'll face on your motorcycle are no different from the situations you'd face in your car. So, once again, there is nothing new here to learn. We go back to the toolbox and dig out our tried-and-true braking habits: smooth, steady, increasing pressure on the brake lever

Sometimes there's just not enough time or space to find an escape route, or there are more factors converging on a situation than you feel you can safely handle, and your best bet is to pull the ripcord and commit to stopping. Stopping is a great skill, but remember, stopping when other vehicles behind you are still moving can leave you in a real pickle.

In a true, full-blown, maximum stop, the vast majority of the work is done with the front brake. On smaller, lighter bikes, the front can do *all* the work if you ask it to.

and the brake pedal, not as much on the rear as on the front. Only now your time and space is compressed, due to the emergency nature of the maneuver. You have to use this smooth, steady, increasing pressure to build up braking pressure very quickly and then continue to increase the pressure until you come to a complete stop, riding right up to the edge of your available traction but not over it. Squeeze that front brake like you'd squeeze the juice out of an orange, and don't give up on it. In an emergency stop, your front brake will do 75 percent or more of the work.

You have to be mindful and well practiced in how *not* to lock up either one of your tires on your big bike. When you're braking at the extremes of traction, in an emergency situation with adrenaline flowing through your veins, it is easy to add a little too much pressure. This is especially true for the rear brake, and this will throw your bike into a skid. We'll talk more about controlling a skid in a moment.

We imagine you're starting to think that this whole theme is getting a little old. Good! We planned it that way. The basics of braking with maximum control are the same in any situation, with just a little modulation thrown in here and there to maximize your efficiency. You need to use the same basic braking fundamentals every time you stop, no matter what, because the repetition, familiarity, and habit are what will save your bacon in an emergency. Proper braking technique has to be second nature.

Emergency braking to stop is a skill that you want to have ready and waiting whenever, and if ever, you have to use it. So it is important for you to set aside time to develop this particular skill because you have to break a long-standing reflex. Most people drive a car way more often than they ride a motorcycle. This means that you have car-driving habits just like you have motorcycle-riding habits. And since most people spend more time in the car than on the bike, the car habits are a little more ingrained than the riding habits. In an emergency-stopping situation in which you don't have time to think, only react, you're likely to fall back on the strongest habit.

So there you are in your car, driving merrily off to the grocery store, and you suddenly have to make an emergency stop: maybe some little kid just rode his bicycle out in front of you. What's the technique? Stomp as hard as you can on the brake pedal, right? Most modern cars have antilock brakes now anyway, and there's very little modulation you can bring to four wheels at once through a little pedal. But this is the habit most people have, and for better or worse, it works for most of them if they're reasonably alert.

But is stomping on the brake pedal of your motorcycle going to work for most people? No, not even close. Also, if you go and stomp on the brake like you do in your car, how do you think you'll treat the front brake lever? I'll tell you what you're going to do, you're going to grab that thing as hard as you can and slam it shut. In a pressure situation, the hand is going to spaz out just like the foot. All of

our good braking skills have just been thrown out the window!

But there are solutions to this problem. First and foremost: ride more! Leave the car at home. Let your most ingrained habits come from your bike and not your car. Then you'll be less likely to revert to car-driving mode in an emergency—you'll always be in the "riding frame of mind." Second: practice and use your brakes the same

To keep your habits and instinctual reactions in motorcycle mode, rather than car mode, ride that bike as often as you can. The less you use a four-wheeled vehicle, the less that mindset is going to pop up in your riding skills.

Simply put, friction is the relationship between the rubber and the road. More specifically, we are interested in the friction at the point where the rubber meets the road. The actual area of contact between the road and the tire is called the contact patch.

way, for every stop, and on every ride—and make sure your downshifting is perfect right along with it. Then the habit of the smooth, steady, increasing pressure squeeze of the front brake lever with the same kind of action but just a little less pressure on the rear brake pedal can become the overriding habit on your motorcycle, regardless of the situation. Finally, pay attention! Emergency-stopping situations don't just pop up out of nowhere (well, *sometimes* they do). Usually there are clues that tell you beforehand, such as an intersection approaching, a "walk" signal change at a corner, or a popular freeway exit coming up and the guy with out-of-state plates is in the left lane. Having good situational awareness means you may never have to use your brakes in an emergency, ever.

Skidding

Skidding is not a technique we want to encourage or practice, but understanding why and how a bike skids will help you develop your traction sense, improve your braking, and allow you to know what to do when and if it ever happens to you.

Before learning how to control a skidding motorcycle, we really do need to talk about the basics of getting a vehicle or a motorcycle stopped.

Stopping any vehicle on a roadway, or any surface for that matter, is all about friction. (Some people prefer the term *traction*. For this discussion, consider the two terms interchangeable.) Simply put, friction is the relationship between surfaces in contact with each other.

Given the importance of the contact patch to our motorcycles (this is the place that makes our motorcycles go forward and stop), we should probably talk a bit more about what it is. Well, it is exactly what it sounds like: the contact patch is the patch on your tire where the rubber is in direct contact with the roadway surface. If you walk out and take a close look at your bike right now, get your eyes down close to the ground, the garage floor, or whatever surface your bike is parked on, and you will see that there is not a whole lot of actual front-to-rear contact surface on your tire. As for the width, it can't be any wider than what your tire is, and in actuality it is a lot less. So, put this length and width of the contact patch together, and you find that it is only a few square inches of rubber actually in contact with the roadway surface.

Given the importance of the contact patch, tire manufacturers

There are only a few inches of rubber on that tire that are actually touching the ground. And these few inches of rubber are responsible for everything you do on your motorcycle, from emergency stopping, to hard riding the twisties, to leaning the bike over as far as you can stand it. This makes the contact patch a pretty important few inches of rubber. *Kawasaki Motors Corp.*

"... you need to make sure that you are not trying to carry too much on your motorcycle, putting more load on the tire than it was designed to carry, and to make sure that you maintain proper air pressure in your tires."

put a whole lot of research into tire compound materials and design. If you want your tires to perform their best for you, especially when you really need them to, then you really need to make sure you use them like the manufacturers tell you to. In other words, you need to be keenly aware of weight and tire pressure. That is, you need to make sure that you are not trying to carry too much on your motorcycle, putting more load on the tire than it was designed to carry, and to make sure that you maintain proper air pressure in your tires. We discussed optimal tire pressure in Chapter 1.

There are a several things that can affect the size of your contact patches. But, in the final analysis, most of these don't really matter. But before we move on to friction and skidding, let's cover just a couple of interesting facts about the contact patch.

The contact patch is a little smaller on a rolling tire than it is on a stopped tire. This means it's even smaller than you thought it was when you looked at it on your parked bike.

Changes in air pressure in the tire change the size of the contact patch. Literally, changes in air pressure inside the tire change how the tire contacts the roadway surface, but the two statements mean the same thing. Too much air or to little air results in tire changes that make the contact patch effectively smaller. Another good reason to make sure you are using the right air pressure.

Tire and wheel size change the size of the contact patch. This makes perfect sense: a wider tire means more contact patch. The larger the diameter of the wheel, the bigger the contact patch. So, does this mean the bigger the contact patch, the better we can stop our motorcycles? Nope. Think about your car. It has four tires in contact with the ground, and each of these tires is way bigger than the tire on your motorcycle.

In fact, when you add up the areas of all four contact patches on a car and compare them with the two contact patches on a motorcycle, the total area of contact can be 10 times bigger than that of a motorcycle. But, somehow, the average motorcycle can still stop faster than the average car. (Scratching your head now aren't you? Don't lose any sleep over this. Accept it for what it is and thank your lucky stars that our motorcycle tires work the way they do.)

Friction

Friction is one of the five basic mechanical forces known in physics. The other four are gravity, the normal force, tension, and an external force. Unfortunately, friction is the least understood of these five forces. This provides a little insight as to why larger contact patches don't stop any better than smaller ones. (Doesn't answer any questions, just gives a little insight.) And because friction is an actual force, it has to follow the basic rules that all forces must follow. What are these rules, you ask? Simple. There are only three of them, and they are known as Newton's Laws of Motion. I know that you are all excited now, looking forward to a deep physics lesson on the little understood force that makes our motorcycles go and stop. Well, not today, sorry about that. You are just going to have to settle for a short and focused explanation of things.

When your motorcycle tires are rolling along the roadway, the contact patch on the tire is constantly changing as the tire surface rolls along on the roadway surface. Although this contact patch between the tire and the roadway is changing, the contact patch and the roadway are actually in a static relationship with respect to each other. That is, there is no actual motion between the contact patch of the tire and the roadway surface. This is one kind of friction, called static friction, and in the case of rolling tires it is sometimes also called rolling friction. In other words, when you are just riding along the roadway enjoying life, static friction is what is happening down at the contact patches.

If the bike is in motion and your tires aren't rolling along, the only other thing they can be doing is sliding along the roadway. If the tire is sliding, the contact patch between the tire and the roadway stays the same as the tire slides along the roadway. The relationship between the contact patch and the roadway is no longer static; the contact patch is actually moving along the roadway. This is known as kinetic friction, which in the case of tires is sometimes called sliding friction. Sliding friction is what is happening at your contact patches when they are skidding along the roadway because you locked up the brakes.

So the tires of your motorcycle are in contact with the roadway surface at the contact patches, and either rolling friction or sliding friction is happening at these patches. Not too bad so far. Unfortunately here is where it gets a little ugly. Remember when we said that friction is a force and has to follow the rules? Now, if rolling friction equals sliding friction, life is really simple—no matter what else happens, the forces on your tires will be the same and your motorcycle will always be in a state of equilibrium. But, you guessed it, the two forces are not equal to each other. It turns out that the rolling frictional force is about 10 percent greater than the sliding frictional force. Since the rolling frictional force is greater than sliding frictional force, a rolling tire will stop a vehicle faster than a skidding tire.

Let's put together what we have right now: at your motorcycle's tires the forces are either rolling frictional force (RFF), due to normal rolling along the roadway, or sliding frictional force

For our purposes, there are only two types of friction: rolling (static) friction and sliding (kinetic) friction. Understanding the differences between the two types of friction will go a long way to helping you understand how a motorcycle behaves when skidding. *Kawasaki Motors Corp.*

(SFF), due to the tire skidding along the roadway. These two forces occur at the tires' contact patches, and these two forces are not equal. So just what does this mean for you and your motorcycle?

In most cases, motorcycle brakes operate independently of each other. Since the front and rear brakes operate with different pedals and levers, this means there can be stopping situations where just the front wheel skids, where just the rear wheel skids, or where both wheels skid. Fortunately, the rules for skidding wheels remain the same, no matter what the situation may be.

Controlling a Skid

Starting with the easiest, a skidding front wheel, the *only* technique is to release the brake as soon as possible. There is nothing "smooth" about this, and there are no other options available. Release the brake immediately. If you don't, you'll no longer be able to steer, which means you'll no longer be able to balance the bike. Of course, once the wheel is rolling again and you've regained traction, reapply the front brake to stop the motorcycle, and with smooth, increasing pressure . . . and maybe not as much pressure as that which got you

> **"In most cases, motorcycle brakes operate independently of each other. Since the front and rear brakes operate with different pedals and levers, this means there can be stopping situations where just the front wheel skids, where just the rear wheel skids, or where both wheels skid."**

Only one thing causes your motorcycle tires to skid: too much pressure either at the foot pedal or the hand lever for the situation. If this happens, then you have gone outside of the good habits you have been working on developing and made a mistake. It's a surprisingly common mistake, but it's still a mistake, and mistakes can lead to crashes unless you get them corrected. Note the locked rear wheel.

into the skid. Remember, it is a smooth, steady, and precise *squeeze*.

If you let the front wheel keep on skidding, the motorcycle will become unstable. The front tire will wash out or slide out, and the motorcycle will go down. This is because the rear wheel, which has RFF, is trying to push through the front wheel, which has SFF and is no longer capable of changing direction. Because the front wheel is no longer spinning, it does not want to stay upright and you can turn the handlebars in either direction. Or, they can be forced to turn in either direction, say, due to a bump in the roadway. Once those handlebars get too far out of line,

there is nothing to hold the forward weight up, and the bike goes down.

As for a locked-up rear tire, that is a very different story. Generally the safest course of action for a skidding rear tire (SFF) is to keep it that way, no matter what it feels like the motorcycle is going to do! Here is the most common situation: a panic stop, you go into car-braking habits rather than motorcycle-braking habits and your right foot stomps on that rear brake pedal, causing the rear tire to skid (SFF) while the front tire is still rolling (RFF).

Because SFF (skidding rear tire) is a lesser force condition than RFF (rolling front tire), the rear tire is going

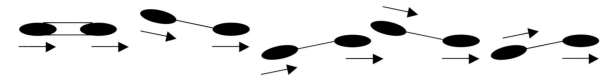

This is what a rear-wheel skid looks like at the tires. The front tire, because it has RFF, is essentially dragging along the rear tire (SFF), much like a trailer swinging behind a towing vehicle.

to swing or oscillate back and forth behind the front tire. The key word here is *behind*. Have you ever been fishing from a moving boat? The boat is trolling along, and you have your line off of the back of the boat, when all of a sudden Moby Dick takes your hook and the fight is on. Old Moby, he wants to get away, so he is swimming back and forth behind the boat, slowing the boat down somewhat, and you're just reeling as best you can to drag him into the boat. Well, this is kind of what it is like on your motorcycle. The front tire has RFF and is pulling the rear tire, which has the lesser SFF, along for the ride. The back tire does not know what to do.

In this situation, that back tire is not going to pass the front tire as long as you keep the handlebars straight, you keep yourself and the motorcycle straight up and down, and you maintain smooth, steady braking on the front wheel. This whole thing is going to feel really weird, and car habits are going to make you want to steer into the skid, but don't do that, the rear wheel cannot and will not pass the front tire, no matter what it feels like!

The trick here is that the motorcycle has to be kept moving forward in a straight line/path of travel, and then it will stop just fine. You maintain a straight line by keeping your head and eyes up, finding a point straight ahead of the front tire, fixing your gaze on that point, and keep the front aimed at that point. This may mean that you have to point toward one side of the road or the other, or deviate from your original or desired

path of travel. (Hope you've got room!) If the motorcycle is steered into the skid, as we're taught to do in a car, or if it's steered around something like an obstacle, the rear tire can and most likely will slide around, and the motorcycle will go down in a lowside crash. Compared to the "other" option, this is not a bad thing at all.

The other option is to release the rear brake so the skidding rear tire starts to roll again. Here we have what we call a highside crash, a "perfect storm" of RFF versus SFF.

Look at the diagram of what the tires are doing during the skid, and look at the direction the arrows are pointing. When the rear brake is released, if the arrows are pointed in the same direction, life is good. The RFF on

The bad side of motorcycle riding. Lots of folks claim that they did it on purpose. But looking at their road rash, it's a little tough to swallow that they volunteered for such treatment.

The highside crash. Wow. The last time I saw someone fly like that it was at the rodeo. It is likely that this crash was caused by the rider spinning up the rear wheel, accelerating out of a turn, but the process and result are more or less the same as a skidding highside.

the front and rear tires is acting along the same line of action at the same time. But, if the arrows are not pointed in the same direction, which is most probably the case, things are about to get real interesting.

Remember, RFF is greater than SFF. When the rear brake is released, the tire bites and immediately starts rolling in the direction that it is pointed, which now is not the same direction as the front tire and definitely is not the same direction it was moving 0.001 seconds ago. Motorcycles are single-track vehicles and cannot move in two directions at the same time. What happens can best be described as follows: the top half of the motorcycle gets driven over the bottom half of the motorcycle, and it goes down in a highside crash, flinging the rider off the bike. A highside is the worst kind

of crash you can have without hitting another object. Generally speaking, potential injuries in a highside are worse than those in a lowside.

That's not to say a lowside crash has all that much better of an outcome. I went down in a braking highside once at about 30 miles per hour. (That's the advantage of being a crash expert, you can go back and completely figure out your own stupid mistakes!) I tore up my gloves and knees of my pants, scuffed up my boots—and never touched my helmet to the ground . . . until my body came to a stop and I needed to rest and take stock of all of my body parts. On the other hand, I went down in a lowside in a sharp right-hand turn at about 3 miles per hour. I hit my helmeted head so hard I swear to you that I saw stars and planets circling around my head like in cartoons.

To sum it all up, if you lock the front wheel, release the front brake right away and reapply it with smooth, steady, and precisely increasing pressure. If you lock the rear wheel, unless you can time the release so that the rear tire is directly in line with the front wheel, keep it locked up and maintain a straight-ahead path of travel along with smooth, steady front braking. If the motorcycle does go down with the rear wheel locked, it will be a lowside crash. If the rear wheel is locked and then released when out of line with the rest of the bike, you'll get a much more severe highside crash. Your best bet is never to let your riding or the situation get to this point: plan ahead and have your skills practiced to the point of being flawless, in any situation.

One last word: this whole skidding discussion was for the majority of motorcycles out there now that have independent and manually operated front and rear brakes. However, there are some other styles of brakes out there, for example, integrated and linked braking systems. These systems can still result in a locked front or rear wheel, so the rules still apply. One other type of braking system that is becoming more and more common is the antilock brake system. These brakes do just exactly what their name implies, no locking up of the front or rear tires. With antilock brakes you don't have to worry about what to do with a locked or sliding front or rear wheel because neither of them will lock up. However, antilock brakes are only for-sure if you're not leaned over or you're not on a heavily sloped surface. You'll always want to avoid steering or leaning during moments of heavy braking, which we'll discuss more in Chapter 10.

Chapter 8

Basic Cornering

**▮ Throttle Management ▮ Countersteering
▮ Where to Look**

This rider may be dressed like a pro, but his body position is all wrong. He's sitting up on top of his bike, rather than leaning into the turn, and it has taken away some valuable cornering clearance.

The techniques you use to throw the bike around at low speeds are quite a bit different from what you do to turn at 15 miles per hour and up. Once you leave the parking lot and hit the road, you're in Countersteering Territory.

Big-bike design is focused more on stability than cornering. The bike is more reassuringly stable and feels more planted at higher speeds. Although twisty roads can be fun, big bikes are generally not designed to slice and dice them. Cornering clearance takes on a new meaning. Turning the bike quickly and nailing the perfect cornering line take significant effort backed up by lots of practice.

But curvy roads are ultimately the ones to which riders of all types of bikes are drawn, so your cornering skills have to be sharp — on a big bike,

the ability to take it dancing in the canyons is 90 percent rider and 10 percent bike.

Fortunately, where the sequence of braking, steering, and throttle were compressed and overlapped at slow speeds in the parking lot, the control inputs in faster turns stretch out in time and space. You have a little bit more room to work. On a big bike, or any bike, you're going to spend the vast majority of your time at higher speeds, so you need to know what you're doing.

Body Position

Body positioning for higher speeds is going to be different than for lower speeds. Masterful high-speed cornering requires a combination of being both rigid and flexible to keep the bike stable and easy to manage.

Opposite: When riding in a large group the possible lines available for cornering become severely limited, necessitating extra caution.

Experts use different body positioning for higher-speed cornering than for low-speed turns. Note how the rider has moved his mass toward the inside of the turn, weighting the inside peg. This provides better control feedback and also increases available lean angle by moving the center of gravity inward.

Your head and eyes should still be "up" and focused on where you want to go, but because your speed has increased, you need to look farther into the distance. You should be looking at least two to four seconds ahead — focusing on where your bike is going to be in two to four seconds.

Just like riding at parking-lot speeds, your knees and thighs are still going to be tight against the motorcycle. Grip the bike with your lower body, and keep your upper body loose and flexible. However, unlike low-speed riding, any weight you shift will be to the *inside* of the turn and not the outside. If you're going to weight a peg, it's going to be the inside peg. If you're going to move

your head, shoulders, or butt, it's going to be to the inside. There'll be more on that later.

What's most different is that at higher speeds, your upper body should be *relaxed*. Riding at slower speeds, you got a real workout using your shoulders, arms, and hands to muscle that bike around. But at higher speeds, your upper body's job is to guide the bike rather than force it. Your shoulders and arms should be loose, flexible, and ready for action. Hold the handgrips like they're a pair of baby birds. Keeping too tight a death grip on the bars will give your bike unwanted and unneeded inputs and interfere with its natural ability to hold a line.

Not that the authors would ever suggest you do this midcorner, but you should be able to take either hand off the handlebars at any time and still be in complete control of the bike. If you're not able to do this, you're holding on to the bars way too tight—which means you need to improve your riding posture.

Throttle Management and Cornering Clearance

For high-speed cornering, good throttle management not only adds to stability but also maximizes traction, cornering ability, and clearance. Just like in low-speed turns, ultrasmooth throttle keeps the bike stable and predictable. But at higher speeds, smooth throttle also balances the bike front to rear, which allows the tires to grip their best, helps the suspension to do its job, and provides maximum cornering clearance—and big bikes with their big, wide floorboards need all the cornering clearance they can get! Decelerating during a turn or being too heavy-handed on the throttle compresses the suspension, lowers the bike to the ground, and reduces cornering clearance.

Your goal while cornering at higher speeds is to have neutral or positive throttle all the way from turn entry to exit. All your slowing, downshifting, and braking should be completed before entering the turn. Build up to higher-speed cornering a little at a time, with lots and lots of practice at slower speeds to learn how far you can lean the motorcycle before touching down hard parts. Something to remember about these hard parts, such as floorboards and side stands: these are your early warning devices. When you start dragging a piece of your motorcycle along the road

Different bikes and different riding positions will result in different cornering clearances. Here we see two bikes at very similar lean angles, but due to the bike design, one bike has plenty of clearance left while the other is already dragging hard parts—even though the rider is leaning more to the inside.

in a turn, you don't have much room left before you have gone a little too far. And a little too far quickly becomes a lot too far. One other thing to remember about cornering: it is always better to come into the corner too slow rather than too fast. You can always add speed through the turn, but you don't always have a chance to take it

away before something bad happens. Stirling Moss once said: "Better to go in slow and come out fast than to go in fast and come out dead." True, that.

Countersteering

Countersteering was, and still is, something of a mystery in the motorcycle world. All riders use countersteering every time they ride, whether they realize it or not. Some riders take it at face value, use it, and ride happily into the sunset. Other riders, usually old timers who have never made any effort to learn about or improve their riding, will shake their heads in disbelief when you try to explain it to them. Still other riders think they understand it, but in reality, they have no idea what they're talking about. They use it and make it work but without knowing exactly what it is they're doing . . . and there is absolutely nothing wrong with that.

Simply put, at speeds greater than a fast walk or jogging speed, countersteering is the most efficient way to get the motorcycle to lean quickly. There are other ways to do this, such as leaning your body first, but any method other than countersteering is inefficient at best and disastrous at worst.

Here's how you do it. If you want the motorcycle to go right, press right. That is, to make the motorcycle turn to the right, you first need to press forward on the right handgrip—initially turning the front wheel to the left. As the front wheel deflects to the left, the motorcycle leans to the right to compensate. Once the desired lean angle for the corner is achieved, you release the pressure enough for the front tire to fall to the right, and the bike goes right.

The same thing goes if you want the motorcycle to go left: press left. Press forward on the left handgrip, the tire deflects to the right, the bike leans left, then the front tire falls to the left and you're cornering the way nature intended—with the front wheel pointed into the turn.

On a bigger bike, depending on its design or how it's set up, it may not actually feel like you are "pressing" the inside handgrip to countersteer. You may feel like you have to "pull" on the outside grip to steer the bike. That's okay. On some bikes, it may even feel like you have to "twist" the handlebars, pressing inside and pulling outside, to get the bike to react the way you want. No matter. However you do it, whatever it takes to countersteer your bike, it's still countersteering, and it still works.

Where most people get it wrong is in thinking that countersteering actually *turns* the motorcycle. Not so. Countersteering only *leans* the motorcycle. Once leaned, the handlebars and front wheel are pointed in the direction of the turn, just like everybody thinks they're supposed to be. It's just that most people don't notice that the front wheel falls into the turn. It feels like they're countersteering constantly.

Once you're leaned over and turning at speed, you can continue to adjust your lean angle by countersteering. If the turn tightens up and you need more lean angle, you press the inside handgrip a little more to get to your new lean angle, then release the pressure just enough to let the front tire fall back into line. On most big bikes, it will feel like you always have to hold pressure on the inside handgrip throughout the entire turn. It feels this way because this is exactly what you are doing to keep your motorcycle leaned over so that it will turn. This is what countersteering and leaning the motorcycle to turn at speed is all about.

Now that you understand countersteering, you can start practicing it on the road, getting the bike to turn quickly and with precision. It helps to

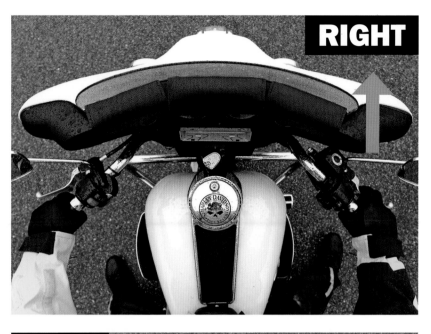

Countersteering means pressing forward on the inside handgrip, pulling backward on the outside handgrip, or some combination of the two, depending on your bike. This initial input turns the front wheel away from the direction of the turn, which leans the bike quickly into the turn. Press right, lean right, go right. Press left, lean left, go left.

continue to ride the same curve or the same section of road over and over, trying different countersteering inputs each time. Over time and with practice, you'll develop a good feel for exactly how much input is required to get exactly the amount of lean you desire and carve the exact line through the turn that you want.

Bike is straight up and down, no countersteering inputs yet.

The rider presses forward on the right handgrip, initially deflecting the front tire to the left.

The bike immediately starts leaning right. Note that the wheel is still pointing left.

As the bike continues to lean, the front tire begins to fall (right) into the turn.

As the bike leans and the turn is begun, the front tire continues to fall to the right, tracking now with the turn.

Once the bike is leaned and is tracking through the turn, the rider continues to countersteer as needed. For more lean and a sharper turn, press more on the right handgrip. For less lean and a wider turn, or to stand the bike up, press the left handgrip.

Line Selection

My favorite rookie question is, "What's the best line through a turn?" Unfortunately, the answer has to be, "Show me the turn, and I'll show you a line." Every turn requires a different line, and every rider will have his or her own idea of the best one.

Most turns can be safely negotiated using the outside-inside-outside path of travel. Every turn also uses a sequence: entry, turn-in, apex, and exit. And every turn requires four steps: slow, roll, look, and press. (Note that this differs from the "slow, look, lean, and roll" or "slow, look, press, and roll"

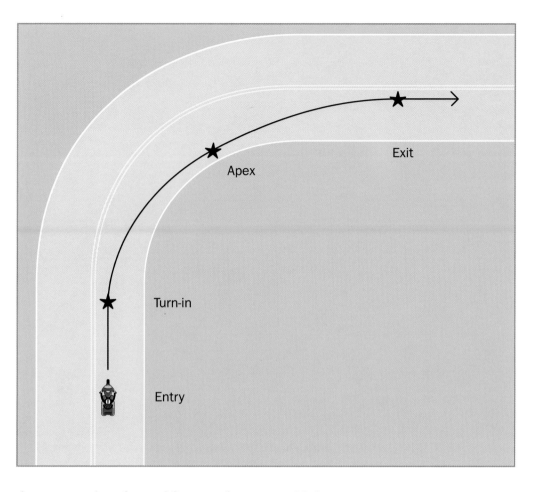

The standard line through a 90-degree corner. The rider sets up on the outside of the turn, sweeps across the inside, and finishes on the outside again. At the entry, speed is set for the slowest part of the turn. At turn-in, the rider countersteers to lean the bike into the turn. The apex for a standard 90-degree turn is at its midpoint. The exit is the point at which the turn straightens out or changes direction.

that you may have learned from another trusted source.) This is a standard cornering line and sequence for new and average riders, and it works just fine in almost every situation.

Riders use the outside-inside-outside line to increase their line of sight and to straighten the curve somewhat. By starting on the outside, a rider is able to look farther through the curve and see what's coming up next: a straightaway, another curve, or an animal or debris in the road. The best advice for the beginning of the turn is to stay as wide as you can for as long as you safely can. By then swinging inside and finishing on the outside, the rider is able to increase the radius of the corner, which requires less lean angle and leaves the most cornering clearance and traction available for surprises. The outside-inside-outside line is the standard line through any corner, whether it's

a 90-degree turn or an increasing- or decreasing-radius curve.

Overlapping the outside-inside-outside line is the sequence: entry, turn-in, apex, and exit. Entry is the point at which the road begins to turn. It is at that point that you should have all your shifting and braking completed and your speed set for the turn. You should be at neutral or slightly positive throttle, set up at the outside of the turn. Turn-in is the point at which you see the exit, countersteer to lean the bike, and set your lean angle and turning radius for the duration of the turn. Ideally, this is one countersteering input rather than several smaller inputs throughout the turn. The apex is the point at which the bike is closest to the inside of the turn. At the exit, the road either straightens out again or starts another turn.

The four steps to cornering are 1) slow, 2) roll, 3) look, and 4) press. Once

In a 90-degree turn, the apex is at the center of the turn. The exit is where you're no longer steering and are more or less straight up and down again, ready for the next turn. In an increasing-radius turn, the apex can come a little earlier. But in a decreasing-radius turn, it is wise to delay both the turn-in and apex—you should not turn the bike in until you know where the exit is!

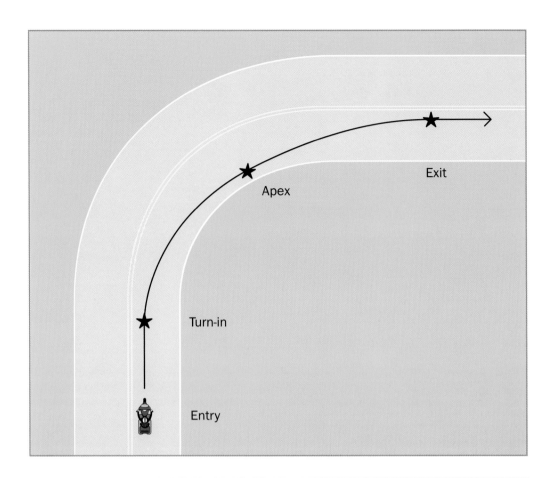

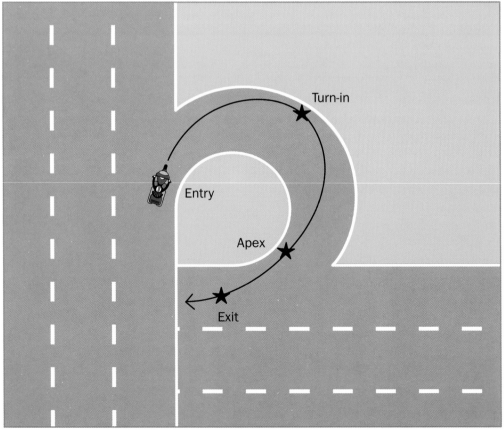

outside of the parking lot, speeds and corners vary so much that your first priority after slowing for a corner is to get the throttle opened up again to get the bike stable. Looking and pressing come later.

1. Slow to a suitable entry speed, which is the speed required to negotiate the tightest part of the turn safely and with something in reserve. All your decelerating, braking, and downshifting should be complete well before the turn entry. Decide at this time the exact point at which the road begins to curve, and plan to turn the bike in at that point.

2. Roll on the throttle, using neutral or positive throttle to settle the suspension so the bike's ready to corner. Don't wait for the turn entry to roll on the throttle. Have your throttle position set and the bike settled before you reach the turn-in point.

3. Look all the way through the turn until you see the exit. If you can't see the exit, then point your nose around the corner where you think the exit might be and just move your eyes to help you see yourself through the turn. Note that you still have not started turning yet. Don't commit to the turn until you know where the exit is. If you can't see the exit, you should assume that it's a decreasing-radius corner and that the turn will tighten up on you before it stretches out again.

4. Press on the handlebars and countersteer the bike into the turn. Make every effort to turn the bike only once, setting yourself up on a nice, smooth, consistent arc that runs the entire length of the turn, from entry to exit.

Traditionally, the turn-in (press) is one steering input. Advanced riders use a later turn-in and a later apex, which improves sightlines and safety margins in blind and decreasing-radius turns (turns in which the radius tightens up near the exit).

Most curves that require decelerating or braking come with an advisory speed limit. This advisory speed limit is well within the corning capabilities of a motorcycle for this corner. However, depending on your skill, comfort and experience, the advisory speed may be too fast (or far too slow!) for you and your bike. Use these advisories as guidelines, they can give you a good place to start for your cornering speed, but don't rely on them for setting the speed that's safe for *you*. (For what it's worth, advisory cornering speeds are based on a vehicle occupant's comfort for going around the turn. It has been decided that about 0.2 g's lateral acceleration is the lowest-common-denominator comfort level for a turn. This is well within the limits of a motorcycle.)

Look all the way through the turn until you see the exit. Remember, setting up to the outside helps you see through the turn and find the exit quicker.

Riding Drill Number 6
SLOW, ROLL, LOOK, AND PRESS

For this drill you need a long, wide parking lot with no obstacles like light poles, etc. Mark two starting points at the two lower corners of the parking lot. About halfway up the parking lot, mark two turning points.

Your objective with this drill is to get the *sequence* of slow, roll, look, and press down to a habit. Just like braking uses the same basic technique for every situation, you'll use this same basic sequence for every corner you ever encounter on your motorcycle, so drill the habits into your brain as hard as you can. Talk to yourself while you're doing it—"Slow . . . roll . . . look and press"—and if you find yourself getting the steps out of order, stop for a moment and think about why.

Do several (5 to 10) turns in one direction before moving to the other side and trying the other direction.

The best part of this drill is that you don't necessarily need a parking lot to practice, you can practice every time you ride, every corner you take. Though it might seem silly, *talk* to yourself out there: SLOW, ROLL, LOOK, AND PRESS, every time.

If you're fairly new to riding or fairly new to riding your particular bike, you should practice this drill away from traffic in a quiet parking lot once a month for your first six months, for at least an hour each time, and maybe once a year in the springtime after that. But, any time you're out riding and feel like you're not cornering very well, it's time to head back to school: get back to the parking lot and reset your cornering baseline so it's drilled into your head again.

Once you've mastered this drill, slow, roll, look, and press will become ingrained in your muscle memory.

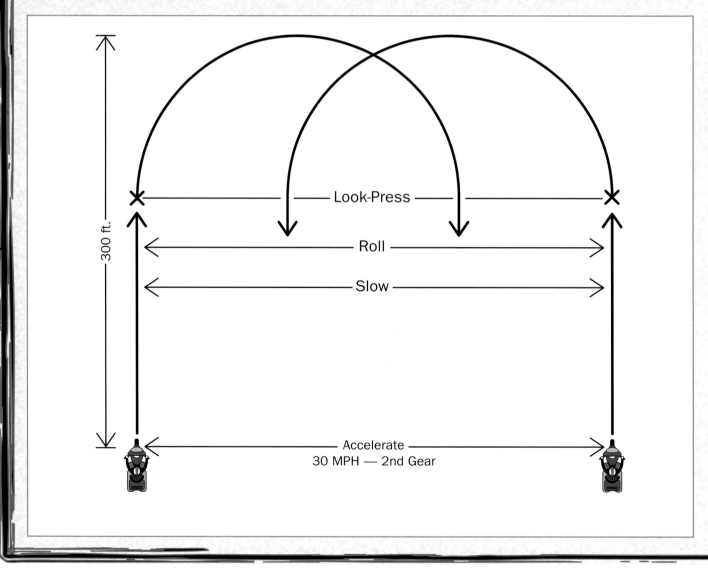

1

2

Start from a stop and accelerate up to 30 miles per hour in second gear. SLOW. Well before you reach your turn marker, use both brakes to slow to an entry speed of about 20 miles per hour. Don't look down at your speedometer. Keep your head and eyes up.

ROLL. Just before the turn marker, roll on the throttle, using either neutral or positive throttle to settle the bike and get it ready to turn.

3

4

LOOK and PRESS. At the turn marker, turn your head 90 degrees and press the inside handgrip to lean the bike.

Keep your head turned, looking two to four seconds ahead of you, and continue to apply positive throttle to accelerate all the way through the turn.

Continue turning until you've done a complete 180 and are heading back toward the starting point again.

5

The rider on the outside will see the exit and the next turn earlier than the rider on the inside. Unless the rider on the inside knows these turns by heart, he's in for a surprise.

The standard line through a 90-degree corner. Slow, roll, and look are all completed near the entry, and press is completed at turn-in.

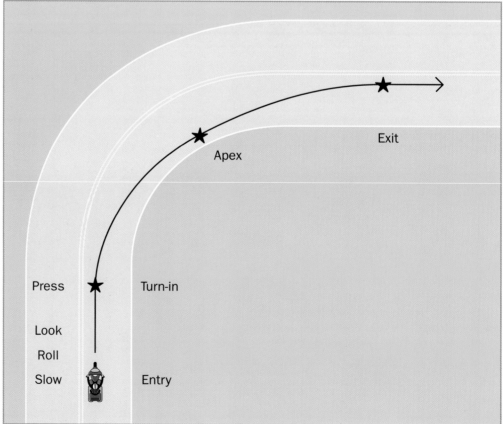

Your reference point is so far in the distance, you could probably safely travel at any speed in which you could stop before the vanishing point.

The point at which the road edges seem to converge is where you should be focused. How far away the point seems indicates how fast you can ride. *Victory Motorcycles*

Your reference point is much closer to you. Your speed should reflect the distance between you and that point. In an emergency, you may need to be able to stop the bike before you get there.

Where to Look

We've already said that you should look at least two to four seconds ahead, as far through the turn as you can, but you're probably asking yourself, "But *where* should I look?" Look for the point in the distance at which the two edges of the road seem to converge, or, in some cases, the place where the road disappears behind a hill, a grove of trees, or some other visual obstruction. This is called the "vanishing point." It's the same as the arbitrary point used in Art 101 classes to teach drawing in perspective.

Simply put, the vanishing point (referred to in *Motorcycle Roadcraft* as a "limit point") is an imaginary point that can help you determine your speed, your turn-in, and your roll-on. In addition to all that, it gives you the direction and approximate distance in which to focus for superior control of the motorcycle. Adjust your speed with respect to how the visual point appears to be moving. If the visual point moves toward you, you should decelerate. If it moves away from you, you can accelerate.

The cardinal safety rule of cornering is that you set your speed such that you are able to make an emergency stop within the amount of road that you can see—you want to be riding slowly enough that you are able to stop before you reach the vanishing point.

As you approach and ride through a corner, the position of the vanishing point will move relative to your position. Sometimes it will move toward you, sometimes away, and sometimes it will seem to be stationary. What it's doing at any given moment tells you what you should be doing at that moment.

Choosing a Line

You won't always be able to use the standard outside-inside-outside, 90-degree corner line. It's an ideal, generic cornering line that makes for a good starting point, but the line you use must be one that you choose, specific to the situation. Some corners will be blind. Others will be strewn with gravel or oil. Some will be decreasing-radius turns that require a later turn-in and apex. You'll have to adapt your standard line to accommodate these hazards.

More advice for cornering lines will be found in the next chapter. Tips and techniques for changing your line midcorner will come in Chapter 10.

Because of the debris on the outside line here, you'll need to adjust your path of travel to the inside, which will require more cornering input.

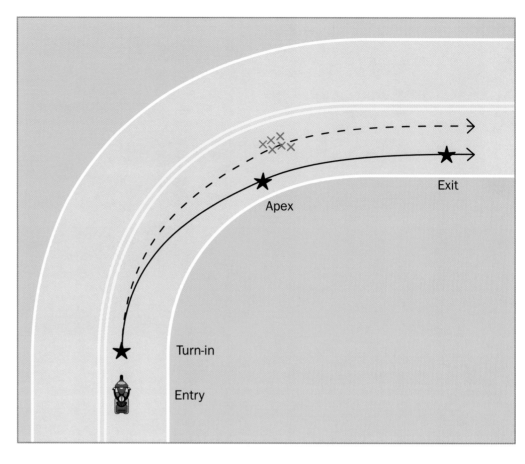

Because of the gravel on the inside of this turn, you'll need to change your line and apex.

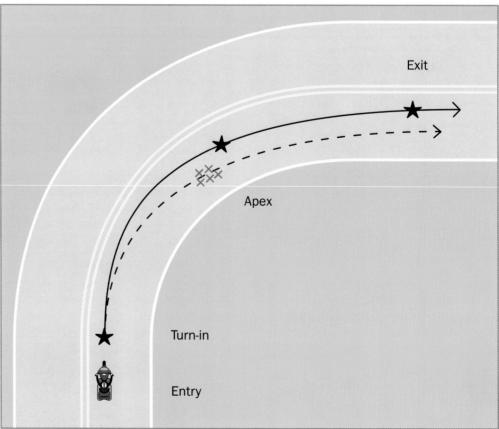

Chapter 9

Advanced Cornering

■ **The Inside Line**

■ **Expert Body Position**

It's a common car-driver mistake to turn in early or cross the centerline at the beginning of a left-hand turn.

roads require a more cautious approach (see Chapter 10).

The standard outside-inside-outside path of travel is fine if there is no risk from oncoming traffic or if the next curve is the same as the last one—a right-hander after a right-hander, for example. But the standard path of travel is not ideal for unpredictable oncoming traffic that may encroach into your lane, or for setting up for the most likely next turn—a left-hander after a right-hander, and vice-versa. The standard outside-inside-outside line can be improved upon for safety, efficiency, and fun.

Safety. In countries where you ride on the right-hand side of the road, if you're going to cross over the centerline, you'll do so usually in the same place: at the beginning of a left-hand turn and at the end of a right-hand turn. (The opposite, of course, is true in those countries that use the left-hand side of the road.) The inside line allows an extra safety margin during the first half of a left-hander and the second half of a right-hander against oncoming traffic encroaching your space.

Efficiency. The outside line is great when the curve ends in a straightaway

Previous page: Once you've got the basics of cornering down, you can adjust your technique to improve your safety, efficiency, and fun factor. The Inside Line works well on all but the roughest, narrowest roads. If the road is wide enough and improved enough to allow for painted lines at the center and outside, it's just begging for an improved technique.

The Inside Line

The Inside Line is an expert cornering line that kicks the whole process up a notch for safety, efficiency, and fun.

The Inside Line uses an outside-inside-*inside* path of travel, which increases your safety margin and provides better positioning for the next turn. The Inside Line works best on wide, well-marked roads with good sightlines (that is, plenty of room to work with and few surprises). Tighter

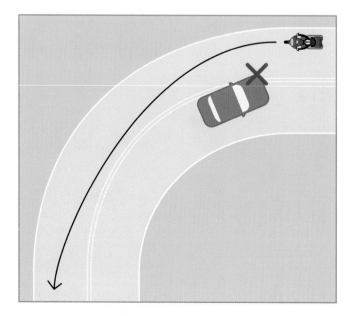

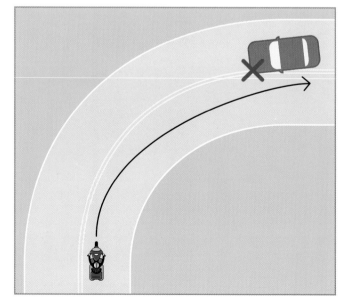

The outside line positions the rider too close for comfort if there's encroaching traffic.

or another curve in the same direction. But that's a relative rarity. There is a tendency in all roadway design that a right-hand curve will follow a left-hand curve, and vice-versa. You're probably wondering, "Just how in the *hell* do they know that?" This is basic grade-school geometry: the shortest distance between two points is a straight line. And the sad truth is, roads are not built for fun, or for scenery . . . for the most part. They're built in the straightest line possible, to go strictly from Point A to Point B. They're all business, no time for chit-chat, get to your destination as efficiently as possible.

Of course the left-right-left-right rule is not absolute, but more often than not, a left-hand turn is going to follow a right-hand turn, and vice versa.

In this sequence, the rider is planning an outside-inside-outside line, which would be fine—if the next turn were not a left-hander. Note the very poor position at the exit. This corner—and every corner like it—would benefit from an outside-inside-inside line, which would set the rider up perfectly for the next corner.

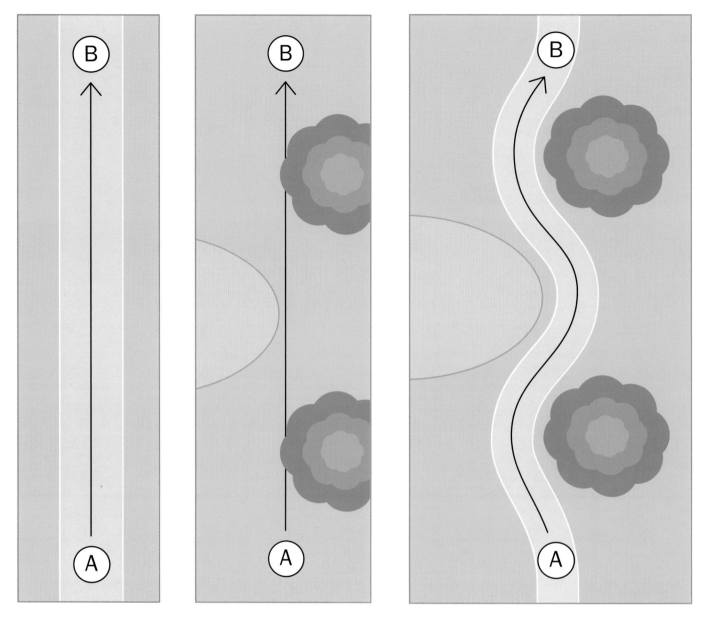

When nature interrupts our plans for a road straight from here to there, highway engineers generally try to adapt to the landscape. This means the road must deviate from its intended path, then correct itself to stay on course. This makes for extra work for the engineers but more fun for the two-wheeled enthusiasts who use these roads.

But a problem arises when the way between A and B is blocked by an obstacle, such as a mountain or body of water. The road has to go over it, go through it, or deviate from its straight line and go around it. Usually, the road goes around it. Then as soon as the road clears the obstacle, it has to deviate again to get pointed back in the right direction. This means when the road cuts left, it needs to cut back to the right to stay on line. Think of this whole process as being like a pendulum. Even though the road is constantly swinging left and right, it's always trying to get back to center.

Fun. The Inside Line has a secret fringe benefit for motorcycle riders. It's a heaping helping of fun! Instead of a large, sweeping arc that effectively straightens an entire turn, the Inside Line gets most of your turning done in

This rider makes these corners look easy. Step one is to set up on the outside of the turn. Speed is set for the slowest part of the turn.

Now the rider has gently opened the throttle and tipped the bike in, and he is looking for his turn-in point.

The rider has found his turn-in point, has turned the bike in hard, and is focused on his exit line.

Note that he still has plenty of cornering clearance, even though he's leaning the bike hard. It is possible that his upper body position is giving him some additional clearance.

As the rider nears his apex, he knows he's found his line and is probably already assessing his speed and position for his entry to the next turn.

The Inside Line has left this rider in a perfect position to attack the next corner with skill and confidence.

Riding Drill Number 7
THE INSIDE LINE

For this drill you need a long, wide parking lot with no obstacles like light poles, etc. Mark two starting points at the two lower corners of the parking lot. About halfway up the parking lot, mark two turning points.

Do several (5 to 10) turns in one direction before moving to the other side and trying the other direction. Practice this drill once per month for at least one hour.

Practicing the Inside Line on the Street

Once you have the corner and these imaginary points committed to memory, it's time to start practicing the Inside Line.

Find a clean, wide, well-marked corner (or series of corners) with good sightlines and relatively free of traffic. Get familiar with the road before attempting to use the Inside Line: make several dozen runs through it, using the standard outside-inside-outside path of travel, until you know every curve by heart. A good place to start looking for these curves is close to home. Remember this is practice to develop your outside-inside-inside lane line. In the first stages of practicing you are not working on how fast you can take

a corner, rather you are working on developing the skill to *use* this kind of line. During the beginning stages your cornering speed is not as important as your cornering placement.

As you get familiar with a corner, start to look for your entry and tip-in point, turn-in point, apex, and exit. The entry/tip-in happens at the instant the road starts to curve. The turn-in is the point at which you can actually see the curve's exit—the imaginary point where the road straightens out. The apex is the point at which your bike will intersect the Inside Line, just a hair before the exit. Draw an imaginary line backward from the exit, straight through the apex—this is the Inside Line. The exit is the point at which the road is no longer curving—it's either straightened out or it's starting to curve the other direction. Entry, tip-in, turn-in, apex, exit. Simple enough?

The Inside Line sets you up for the *most likely* next turn—a right-hander following a left, or a left-hander following a right. If the next turn is another right-hander following a right, or another left-hander following a left, all you need to do is widen your line by easing up on the steering or opening the throttle more or earlier.

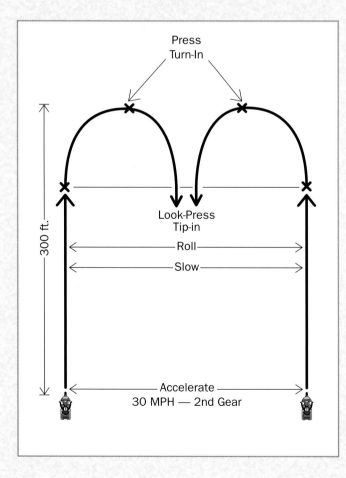

1

LOOK and PRESS. At the turn marker, turn your head 90 degrees and tip the bike in. Keep your head turned, looking two to four seconds ahead of you, and continue to apply positive throttle to accelerate all the way through the turn.

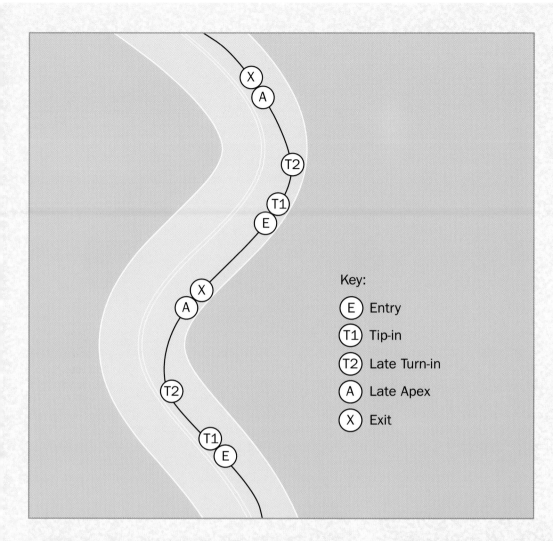

A bird's-eye view of the Inside Line. If it looks as if the line "squares off" the corners, you're right. The turn-in is compressed to minimize the amount of time you're at maximum lean angle and to give you a late turn-in and a very late apex. Note that the entry and tip-in are almost simultaneous. This is also true of the apex and exit. This is an expert cornering technique that will pay big dividends in efficiency, safety, and fun!

Key:

E — Entry

T1 — Tip-in

T2 — Late Turn-in

A — Late Apex

X — Exit

About halfway through the arc, turn your head farther, look all the way back to the other side of the parking lot, and turn the bike in hard, imagining you're aiming for the apex and exit. On the street, decide where you want your exit to be, then hang out wide and wait for it as long as you safely can.

Continue turning until you've done a complete 180 and are heading back toward the starting point again.

All the standard posture requirements are here: good head turn; shoulders, arms, and elbows loose; and gripping the bike with the legs . . . uh, leg. There's no good reason to be riding this hard on the street, but if you're going to kick it up a few notches, it's best that you know how to use your body to buy you more cornering reserve.

a more limited space, which requires more cornering forces, which generates more fun factor.

What makes the Inside Line different from a standard cornering line is, of course, that it finishes on the inside of the turn rather than the outside. But also, the Inside Line uses two cornering inputs: a tip-in and a turn-in. The tip-in is just enough of a steering input to keep you riding parallel to the outside of the curve. The turn-in is a major steering input that takes you from the outside of the curve to the inside. The simplest way to describe the Inside Line is that you're *changing lane positions from the outside of the lane to the inside of the lane, and you're doing it midturn.* The Inside Line requires a very late turn-in and a very late apex. In fact, when done correctly, the apex and the exit are often simultaneous.

"Expert" Body Position

Now comes a chance for you to develop your own personal style. Standard body position is just that—it's standard. Every rider should more or less be using the head-and-eyes up, arms-and-elbows-loose, knees-tight body position. But there are a few ingredients you can add to this cocktail to make it totally your own. Instead of just leaning with the bike into corners, you can use your body position to move the center of gravity inward and add to your cornering clearance. This will allow you to get more reserve out of the same corner—or increase your speed, whichever floats your boat.

A word of advice: unless you're practicing/learning this technique on a closed course (such as a racetrack), build up to this new body position a little at a time—over a period of days or weeks. Don't try everything at once. Just try individual, slight movements, one at a time, and get used to using them before moving on to something else. The distraction of body-position adjustments while also trying to control a big bike in traffic, or before you have your corning line skills down, could easily upset your life-expectancy apple cart, so build up and add these things gradually, just like we mentioned in Chapter 1.

Expert riders lean *into* the turns when they corner. That means they lean their heads, shoulders, and butts *more* than the bike. The purpose for this is to swing the center of gravity inward to reduce the bike's lean angle. This allows them to corner faster—or maintain a better traction reserve.

Start with your head. You should get used to using your head before you try using any other part of your body to reduce your lean angle. (Good advice on many levels!) Just before you initiate the turn-in, press your face toward the inside handlebar. Racers often describe it as "listening to the turn." Point your ear toward the inside of the corner and pretend it's telling you a story. Don't get confused here; point your ear toward the inside of the curve, not toward the ground on the inside of the curve. Keep your eyes level so that you can keep a level horizon in front of you and better judge angles and distances.

Next come the shoulders. Once you've gotten used to pushing your head to the inside, lean in with your shoulders too. Your upper body has quite a bit more mass than your head alone, and this will change your center of gravity and require slightly less of a lean angle.

Last comes your butt. Your lower body has even more mass than your head or your shoulders, so this can affect your lean angle even more. Slide your rear end to the inside of the turn—position your "centerline" on the inside edge of the bike's seat—sort of the opposite of counterweighting.

With all three of these things in place—head, shoulders, and butt—the weight you're placing toward the inside of the turn will reduce the lean angle your bike requires for that turn, allowing you a bigger safety reserve or the ability to corner faster, whichever you're trying to achieve.

This rider uses aggressive body position to gain cornering clearance and control—all while making it look fun and effortless.

Chapter 10

Avoiding Hazards

**▌Typical Hazards ▌Swerving
▌Mid-corner Corrections**

In a situation like this, if a car pulls into your path, swerving should be your last option. If you misjudge another driver's actions, or if the driver changes his or her mind, you could be stuck in an even worse situation. Ideally, brake first to buy yourself some breathing room, then swerve if you have to.

In the last two chapters, we've dealt mostly with controlling the bike in situations that the rider created. But in that great big world out there, you'll find situations nearly every day that you do not create, yet you still need to use your skills and know-how to manage them. Whether it's another vehicle, another "road user" like a pedestrian or animal, or a problem with the road surface, you now have the tools to deal with these hazards, it's just a matter of knowing which ones to use and when.

The tools you've developed throughout the rest of this book that we can now apply to avoiding hazards are your braking skills and your countersteering ability. When you've developed coordinated fine-muscle control and good feel for your brakes, you should be able to use them to make minor adjustments to your speed, major adjustments to your speed, and everything between. And if you are comfortable and confident with your countersteering—you can use firm and precise handlebar inputs to change your path of travel—the art of swerving is just another technique to learn and practice.

There are three rules to follow when dealing with unplanned hazards on the road: 1) adjust your speed before all else, 2) swerve only when you have to, and 3) separate braking from swerving. These rules are 100 percent about safety.

Adjust your speed before all else. This can mean both accelerating to leave a problem behind and braking to create space and time to let a problem dissipate. For the purposes of this book, we're going to stick to talking about

Opposite: Unfortunately, riding on the street also means dealing with predictably unpredictable obstacles to your path of travel or plans for the day. Swerving (and being able to change your speed or line midcorner) is another key to maximum control.

There's not enough tire to handle both braking and swerving at the same time. If you're going to brake, brake first, then swerve. If you're going to swerve, wait until you've completely finished the swerve and are straight up and down again before applying your brakes.

braking. In any bad situation on the road, reducing your speed is the easiest and quickest way to minimize a problem. Often, alert riders can detect a problem brewing and make sure they're nowhere near it when it comes to a head. Reducing speed gives everyone on the road more time and space to interact safely, and it also reduces potential impact speeds, so if it all goes totally wrong, you stand a better chance of walking away.

Swerve only when you have to. This rule ties directly into braking. If braking is your first reaction to a hazard, it leaves you the option of releasing the brakes and swerving if you have to. Not so the other way around. If you decide to swerve around a potential hazard at, say, 50 miles per hour, and the hazard decides to

change its speed or direction, you can't go back and decide to brake instead. You're into it now. Swerving puts you at a point of no return; it puts all your eggs in one basket with no hope of changing your plan if the situation changes.

Separate braking from swerving. Due to the way a motorcycle handles and the tires' finite amount of traction, the fact is, a bike cannot handle being braked and swerved at the same time. Heavy braking uses up all the bike's available traction. Aggressive swerving also uses up all the bike's available traction. Thus, riders have to choose one or the other. If they try to do both at once, depending on the timing of the different inputs, the bike will either tuck the front and crash, skid the rear and lowside, or skid the rear and highside (if the rider makes *all* the wrong decisions.) This goes for riders with antilock brakes too. ABS is designed to use all of the available friction. If you try to swerve when you're heavy on the brakes, you'll meet the same fate as the riders with traditional braking systems. In general, it is best to separate any braking from any cornering as well, but there is a bit of wiggle room there. We'll talk about that a little later.

Typical Hazards

There are two general types of situations in which you will have to avoid a hazard: in a straightaway and in a corner. On the straights, riders often have to deal with other vehicles pulling out in front of them, wild animals looking for food or romance, and road

debris like liquids, sand, gravel, and various objects. In the corners, most often we have to deal with road debris like sand, gravel, dirt, or a combination of these. There can also be wild animals or other vehicles encroaching your lane, either in your direction or opposite your direction, and they can be moving slowly, they can be not moving at all, or they can be moving slowly and then make a sudden turn or stop.

Trick number one is to try and decide beforehand (before you even leave your driveway!) whether you'll swerve or brake in these various situations. We discussed this in the Introduction. Use mental practice and planning for these situations so your immediate, instinctive reaction is more likely to be the best one. Of course,

> **"In the corners, most often we have to deal with road debris like sand, gravel, dirt, or a combination of these."**

In one of the most famous photos in Internet-land, this rider has made one or more serious mistakes and is about to lose some skin.

each situation is different, and there are no hard-and-fast rules. Generally, though, any problem on a straightaway is best dealt with through braking, or sometimes braking and then swerving. As we said before, swerving as a first choice doesn't leave you a whole lot of options and should be used only as a last resort. Problems in corners are best handled with countersteering to change your position and path of travel, and often countersteering must be combined with braking in order to make it work. This is why we say ride at 80 percent and always have that 20 percent in reserve for the unexpected.

Straight Line Maneuvers— Swerving

Well, I guess we should get swerving out of the way. Swerving is a viable option when the object that poses a

hazard has no chance of moving, or the situation is clearly one in which all the other players are completely predictable and your swerve maneuver won't get upended by a new development. For example, there's absolutely no need to slam on your brakes for every turtle crossing your path. There's no need to slam on your brakes for every pothole, freeway couch, or wet spot. A minor, temporary change in your path of travel should solve the problem.

In Chapters 8 and 9 we discussed countersteering for cornering. Swerving is just a special kind of countersteering: instead of using one handlebar input in one direction to lean the bike and turn, swerving uses two consecutive inputs, one left and one right (or vice versa), to quickly change the bike's path of travel but continue the same direction. Keep your head and eyes focused well

You never know what's around the bend. It could be a car over the centerline or a big wash of sand or mud. Decide beforehand what your reaction should be for every situation so that the "correct" response is always the one that's right there at the top of your mind.

Swerving doesn't have to be dramatic. It's just two quick countersteers: one to deviate from your path of travel and one to continue in your original direction. Use a swerve to deal with non-moving objects.

ahead (and *not* on the obstacle), press on the handlebar firmly to lean the bike and alter its line, then press the other handlebar just as firmly to straighten the bike and continue on the new line. Note that the degree of swerving relies as much on the *duration* of the handlebar input as it does the *force* of the input. You can't just stab-stab the handlebars and expect any great correction—that's maybe enough to avoid the aforementioned turtle. You need to press-hold, press-hold to get the direction change you want. And as we said before, do not attempt to combine either of these maneuvers with any braking whatsoever.

You can practice this in a parking lot or on a deserted street easily enough. Find a speed that seems safe and comfortable to you, 20 to 30 miles per hour, and imagine you're riding along in a straight line at a much faster speed, say 50 miles per hour. Now imagine someone's brand-new refrigerator topples off the back of a truck in front of you. Quickly pick a direction you want to swerve, press the handlebar in that direction, swerve four to six feet off your line, then press the other handlebar to recover and continue on straight ahead, imagining the fridge slipping by just to one side of you.

Riding Drill Number 8
SLOW, SWERVE, AND GO

Imagine a situation where you're in heavy traffic. Suddenly, a vehicle pulls out in front of you, sees you, and stops—right in your path. You don't know what the other driver is going to do next, but you know you can't continue on with your intended path of travel, and you know you can't stop—there are too many other cars right behind you who are just as surprised, and probably not as skilled, as you are.

This drill uses an approach similar to Riding Drill Number 5. Again, for this drill, start off *slowly* and build yourself up to greater speeds. You'll need a fairly long stretch of asphalt, at least 300 feet. Identify a mark somewhere in the middle of your overall distance. This is where the imaginary object you're going to swerve to miss is located. Ride toward your mark, and as you approach it, pick your spot to start braking. Once you slow to about 10 miles per hour, swerve around your obstacle (press-hold, press-hold) and then continue forward. How was that? Too easy? Next time through wait a little longer to brake and see what happens. Too difficult? Next time through, brake a little sooner. Evaluate each pass to see how it felt. You don't want this to be an *easy* maneuver—you want to push yourself a little bit—but remember, the important thing is just getting the braking *separated* from the swerve. Make sure you practice at a speed that every time you do it, you do it right.

Each time you start a lap, try braking just a little bit harder than the time before. Once down and back is one lap. Try to do at least four to six laps in a row, then take a short break and think about what you did. Once you're comfortable with 25 miles per hour, bump it up to 30 to 35 miles per hour in fourth gear. Move the markers farther apart if you need to, but don't feel obligated to move them closer together as your skill improves. Don't cut it too close. What's really important here is that you're able to brake hard to deal with a hazard, and completely separate your swerve from your braking. You should practice this drill once a month for at least an hour.

WARNING: We like the idea of making drills realistic because that makes things closer to the way they are on the street, which builds better skills. But this is not a drill you want to make realistic. Don't be tempted to park your car or truck partially out in the roadway, or put a big object or obstacle down in front of you to swerve around. Things don't always work out the way you want them to, and this is only practice. If something doesn't quite go as planned, you don't want to be running into something and crashing. (Try explaining running into your own vehicle to your insurance company!) If you need to have something in front of you to help you visualize, put a big X on the ground with tape. That way if something unexpected happens, you just run over the X and try harder next time.

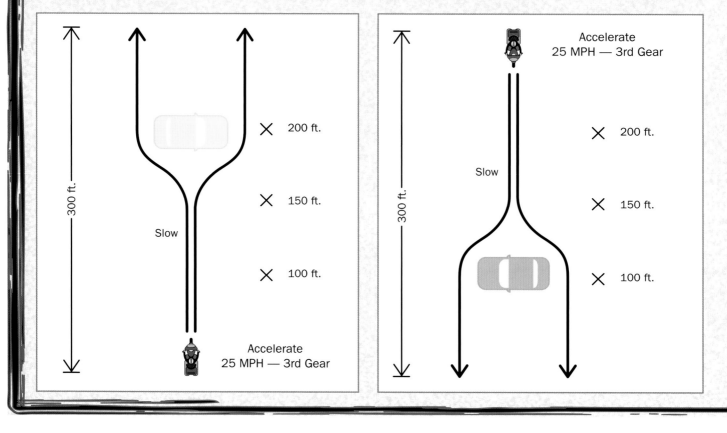

Start from one end and accelerate up to about 25 miles per hour in third gear. When you reach your first mark, start braking, using correct riding posture and braking technique (Chapters 6 and 7), as if you are going to stop *before* you reach the next marker.

Brake down to about 10 miles per hour, downshift to second gear, then release the brakes completely and swerve around the second mark. Be absolutely certain not to initiate the swerve until you've completely released your brakes.

Figure the car that's in your way is 14 feet long, so your swerve should move you left or right by at least 10 feet from your original path of travel.

Think of it as changing lanes, using the shoulder, or using the oncoming lane to get the space you need.

Keep your head and eyes focused on your "escape route," not on the obstacle itself. Quickly swerve to the left or right, then resume your original direction at 10 miles per hour. Once the swerve is complete and the bike straight up and down again, roll on the throttle (imagining the screeching tires behind you) and ride smoothly away.

Slow down and stop at the end of the line, make a quick U-turn, and try it again in the other direction.

> "When the going gets really rough, and it sometimes does, there will be times that you'll need to brake hard down to 10 miles per hour or so . . . and then swerve to leave the hazard behind you and continue on your way."

To get the clearance you'll need, plan to swerve at least four to six feet off your original path. This will put your bike on a safe line to avoid an object and also allow enough room for the sides of your bike, feet, and legs to clear the object too.

One thing to note about swerving is that it's a much quicker maneuver than countersteering through a corner. This means that you don't have time to lean your body with the bike. Your posture should remain straight up and down, and you should let the bike swerve underneath you. Otherwise, your body position is the same as for all other types of riding: head and eyes are up and focused on your desired path of travel, your shoulders and arms are loose, your hands have a light, firm grip on the bars, and you're holding onto the bike with your legs. This will allow you to make quick, precise swerves without too much drama.

Straight Line Maneuvers— Emergency Braking, Then Swerving

Remember, swerving at speed doesn't leave you any other options. For a non-mobile object like a freeway couch, swerving is generally safe. For a moving object, such as a car pulling out in front of you, it's smarter to scrub off speed first, which leaves your options open either to slow more, stop completely, or slow and then swerve. You never know what that car is going to do next, or quite where it's going to end up, so your best bet is to reduce your speed first, to buy yourself some time and space either for the car to clear out or for you to decide what to do next.

Like we said in Chapter 7, rarely if ever does a motorcycle rider need to come to a complete stop in an emergency. If you did an emergency stop every time a car pulled out in front of you, it'd take you all day just

to get to work! So you'll find there are lots of opportunities to brake to minimize a hazard without stopping. When the going gets really rough, and it sometimes does, there will be times that you'll need to brake hard down to 10 miles per hour or so (just like we did in Chapter 7) and then swerve to leave the hazard behind you and continue on your way.

Midcorner Corrections

Well, we've spent all this time telling you how you shouldn't ever combine braking and swerving. And you shouldn't. But what about braking and cornering? Here's where we have a bit of a gray area. It is *possible* to brake successfully while cornering, or to corner while braking, if your skills are very, very good. Your inputs must be smooth and precise, and you cannot already be at the limit of traction. In general, you should avoid braking while cornering or cornering while braking if at all possible. But that doesn't mean you can't, and that doesn't mean you won't have to someday. Once again, here is where riding at 80 percent and having 20 percent up your sleeve can save your biscuit.

Why would you ever want to brake in a corner? For the reasons we described earlier, such as for road debris, wild animals, or other vehicles hogging your lane. Or maybe a turn surprises you and tightens up. These are all situations in which reducing speed will probably help. Then there are other situations, such as a stop sign at the bottom of a curved exit ramp. In this case, you have no choice but to brake while cornering. So obviously it's possible, but what's the technique?

Slowing while cornering requires that you balance traction needs between your braking and your steering. As you're leaned over into a corner, your tires are using up some or all of their available

Sometimes the road itself forces you to brake while cornering. The trick is to use your brakes gently and gradually, applying more braking as the bike straightens up more.

traction, depending on how close to the edge of traction you ride. If you need to add braking into the equation, and keep everything else equal, you need to reduce your lean in order to brake. Or, conversely, if you're braking hard and need to steer, you need to reduce the pressure on your brakes first. And in both of these cases, you can only add in the new input (braking or steering) to the same or a lesser degree that you reduced your lean angle or braking. Or to say this another way, if you are braking and you let up on the brakes a little bit, then you can lean your motorcycle into the turn—just a little bit. If you are leaning into the turn and

you straighten the bike up a little bit, then you can brake—just a little bit.

Unfortunately, there is no hard-and-fast rule for how much you can brake while leaning, or lean while braking. It's dynamic and nonlinear: the more you lean, the less you can brake; the more you brake, the less you can lean, but the tradeoff is not one-for-one. The closer to the extremes you are, the less predictable it gets. Plus, it's obviously going to be different for every bike, every set of tire pressures, every set of suspension settings, and every road surface. We might have said this once or twice before, but we are going to say it again: if you always ride at no more

Experts can start turning before their braking is complete, especially racers who ride at 100 percent. When these riders originally begin their braking, they give it everything they've got in a straight line. But as they approach the turn, they inevitably ease off the brakes and modulate to time their entry perfectly. As soon as the braking goes from 100 percent to something less than that, they've got room to start turning the bike—only a little at first, but as the braking pressure continues to ease, they can continue to turn more and more. Somewhere, midway through the corner, they've completely let off the brakes and are now turning as hard as they can. The transition was seamless to on onlooker, but it demands superior skill and 100 percent attention to pull it off.

than 80 percent, in theory, you always have 20 percent to work with in an emergency. (Yes, it's that important.) Beware, though, if you go past that 100 percent, you'll either be in the air or on the ground.

Resetting Your Lean Angle

Speed and lean angle are inseparable when it comes to cornering. The faster you take a corner, the more you'll have to lean the bike. The slower you take the corner, the less you'll have to lean the bike. You generally can't

reduce your lean angle to any significant degree and still make the corner unless you also reduce your speed.

If you're riding at 80 percent or less, you have room to adjust your lean angle or change your line slightly without slowing. If an oncoming car is straddling the centerline, you can turn tighter (or wider) to put more space between you and the other vehicle. Remember from Chapter 9, the most likely place in North America to see an oncoming vehicle in your lane is at the end of a right turn or at the beginning of a left turn. When

It's not uncommon to find other drivers hogging your lane midcorner. If you're riding well within your limits, you can adjust your line in or out to create more space between you and the other vehicle. On right turns, you need to be mindful not to turn too tightly and run off the inside of the road. On left turns, remember that once you're clear of the car, you've still got a corner to complete, and you'll need to turn quickly and quite a bit harder to make it!

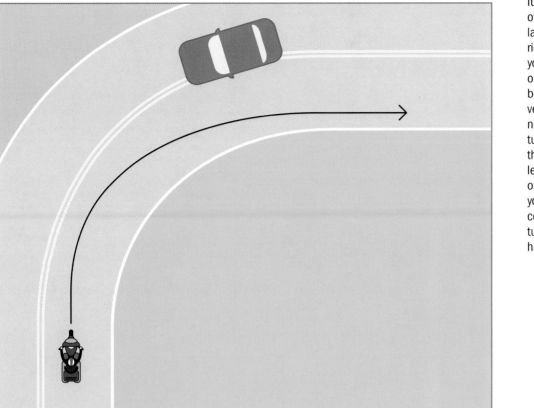

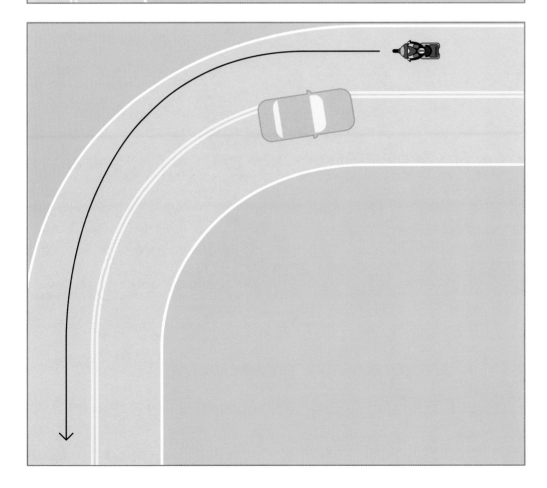

Riding Drill Number 9
CHANGE YOUR LINE

Your objective with this drill is to be able to adjust your line a few feet left or right while in midcorner. This drill uses the same basic layout as Riding Drill Number 6: Slow, Roll, Look and Press. You'll need a long, wide parking lot with no obstacles like light poles, etc. Mark two starting points at the two lower corners of the parking lot. About halfway up the parking lot, mark two turning points. And somewhere near the center of your turning arc, lay down an X with chalk or tape (or use a cone).

1. Start by practicing the sequence of slow, roll, look and press several times, aiming to ride right over the X.

2. Once the basic turn is familiar in both directions and you can pretty much nail the X at will, challenge yourself: aim initially for the X but then imagine there's a wash of gravel right on your line. Widen or tighten your line to go around the imaginary gravel so that instead of hitting the X, your line will pass three to five feet to the inside or outside of it.

Extra credit. Once you're able to widen or tighten your line easily, try to regain your original line by changing your line again: once you've "avoided the gravel" and established a new line, try to tighten or widen your line again to resume your original path of travel.

Alternate drill. Instead of changing your line to avoid the X, change your lean angle instead. Imagine that the area surrounding the X, a six-foot-diameter spot, is wet or sandy. Approach the X normally—at a lean, rolling on the throttle—but as you cross the wet/sandy "area," stand the bike up to reduce your lean angle, and use a slightly more neutral throttle position (do not decelerate, though). As soon as you've cleared the X, countersteer and lean the bike into the turn again, regaining your original line.

One nice feature of this drill is that you don't necessarily need a parking lot. You can practice anytime you come across a nice, clean, wide corner. Even so, you should practice this drill in a parking lot at least twice per riding season for one full hour or for at least two full hours while out riding.

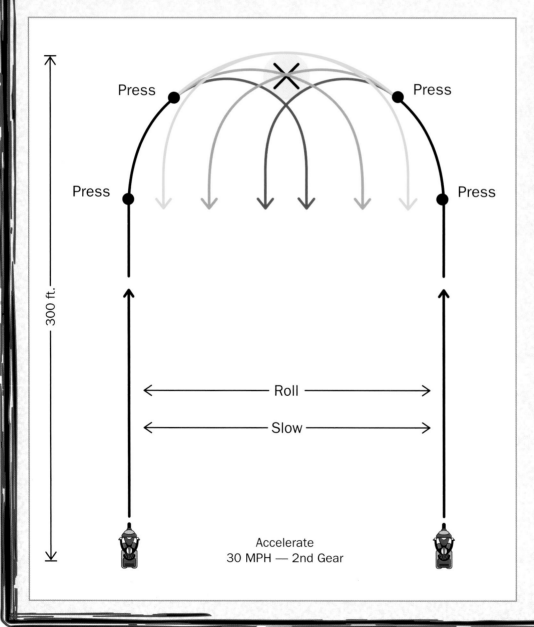

1

Make several passes until you're confident you're following the same line and hitting the same marker every pass. This is your imaginary "ideal" line.

2

When you're ready to begin changing your line, start out each pass following your "ideal" line, then change your line (wide, in this photo) mid corner to accommodate an imaginary hazard.

3

Here the rider makes a smooth arc along his imaginary "ideal" line.

4

To change your line wide, press on the outside handgrip to stand the bike up, then press the inside handgrip—countersteer—to get the bike turned in again. To change your line to the inside (as in this photo), press the inside handgrip, and once past the imaginary hazard, release pressure on the inside grip or dial in some pressure to the outside grip to regain your original line.

Riding Drill Number 10
TURN, BRAKE, TURN

Your objective for this drill is to separate braking from turning. This drill uses the same layout as Riding Drill Number 9: Changing Your Line. Imagine this situation: you're cornering normally, you have the bike turned in, and you realize the corner is tighter than you anticipated. In most cases, if you're riding at 80 percent or less, you can overcome this problem by leaning the bike more and focusing on where you want to go.

But in this case, we're going to say that your path is blocked by fallen rocks, and there's no way you're going to make it unless you scrub off some serious speed and go around it. When you realize you're going to have to brake hard, press the *outside* handgrip to straighten quickly, square up the handlebars, brake hard down to 5 miles per hour or so, then throw the bike back into the corner (low-speed sharp turn).

Safety First: Beware that this sequence has you cornering hard, braking hard, and turning hard, all in the space of a few seconds. Take it *slowly* the first several times and make absolutely sure that you're separating your braking actions from your turning actions. And make damned sure that you have learned this technique and are *completely* comfortable with it at slow speeds before you ramp it up.

1. Start by practicing the sequence of slow, roll, look and press a few times, aiming to ride right over the X. The first several times you practice this, do it rather slowly—15 to 20 miles per hour tops, second gear max.

2. Once the basic turn is familiar in both directions and you can pretty much nail the X at will, it's time to add the braking. Imagine there's a pile of boulders completely covering your lane. Immediately straighten the bike up, square the handlebars, and use maximum braking in a straight line, downshifting to first.

3. In the real world, you may have to stop the bike completely before you can continue. Other times you may be able to make a quick swerve around the obstacle. Either way, when you've finished your braking, you should be straight up and down, balanced, in control, in first gear. Release the brakes completely, ease the clutch into the friction zone, and make a tight turn, going around the imaginary boulders.

Extra credit. As you practice this drill and get used to separating braking from turning, you'll probably notice that straightening the bike in a curve can point you into the ditch or into the oncoming lane—especially if you're using the Inside Line for cornering. This is sad but true. To minimize (but not necessarily eliminate) this, before you straighten the bike, quickly countersteer harder into the turn—*tighten* your turn, move to the inside—for a brief second to buy yourself a tiny bit of extra room. This technique is almost like making a tiny swerve to the inside before you straighten the bike up to brake.

1

2

3

This rider has run wide and is desperately trying to make the corner. He's trying to look through the turn, and applying some braking, to get the bike slowed enough to finish the corner. When this happens, it's rarely pretty, but sometimes ugly and upright is better than pretty and in the bushes.

Note that in real-world situations, you never want to get to the point where you have to use this skill. You want to always be thinking and looking far enough ahead that you're not surprised by anything. But it's still a terrific skill to practice so that the techniques are there when you need them. You should practice this drill twice every riding season for at least one hour or for at least two full hours while out riding.

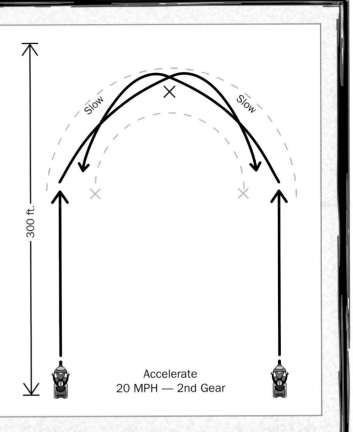

The rider has identified a reason to change his path of travel. With the wet asphalt, there's very little room for error. Best to scrub off some speed.

First, straighten the bike so you can apply brakes to reduce speed. Once the brakes are released, find the best position to finish the turn. Turn the bike in again on a line that makes more sense for the situation. Note that this maneuver has the potential to put you into oncoming traffic (or the ditch). It's better to not let yourself get into this situation in the first place.

faced with this, you have little choice but to use your handlebars to countersteer quickly to adjust your line — keeping your eyes on the road ahead and not on the car's hood ornament!

But probably the most common reason to brake while cornering is when you encounter something on the road surface: water, sand, gravel, whatever. In many cases, these hazards are negotiable at a slower speed and reduced lean angle. It's rare that you'll want or need to stop for every surface hazard, so in these instances, it is a good idea to know how to reduce your lean angle quickly in midcorner.

There are two ways to reset your lean angle while cornering. Which you use depends on how much speed you need to scrub off. The first method is to slow *while* leaning by decelerating or applying the brakes *gently* as you reduce your lean angle. Maybe the corner was just slightly tighter than you thought it would be, or there's a minor amount of gravel to contend with, but nothing that's going to cause you to slide out if you take it a little slower. This technique works when you need only a minor adjustment to your speed and lean angle, and it only works if you are not already at maximum lean.

Another method is to straighten the bike completely, apply maximum braking in a straight line, and then stop . . . or lean the bike again and finish the turn. Slowing is the safest technique in most cases because it allows you to reduce your speed and gives you time to evaluate the hazard further. Straightening the bike also allows you the option of stopping completely if you need to. This method also requires a lot of time and a lot of space, and it requires you to be cognizant of who might be right behind you. Use this technique as a default "go-to" or when you don't know enough about the hazard to risk it.

There is a third method that's fairly tricky but works okay in situations that require only a minor adjustment. When you see a surface problem, turn the bike hard before you get there, which tightens your line. Then, stand the bike up as you ride through the hazard. Once you're clear, immediately turn the bike hard again. This method is appropriate only when you have no other traffic to deal with and you have lots of roadway to work with. And to be honest, it can look pretty ugly: aaagh! turn-turn-turn, straighten, clench buttcheeks, aaagh! turn-turn-turn again. Not for the faint of heart!

Appendix A
Lifting a Motorcycle

Well, now you've gone and done it. Maybe it was a simple tip-over while you were practicing; maybe it was a simple tip-over in a parking lot or at a gas station. Maybe it was something a little less simple, perhaps a poorly planned corner or botched braking maneuver. Either way, you've made a mistake, and now you've got to pay your dues. Don't be too hard on yourself. We *all* do it.

Picking up a motorcycle can be dangerous and cause serious injury if done incorrectly or under poor footing. A bad angle or hurried decision could cause a back injury that could change your life! Always try to get help first—and remember, you don't want anybody else to get hurt either. You need to think clearly, use common sense, and be in good physical condition to wrestle one of these big mothers back up into standing position. Keep your body and back straight, and lift only with your legs. Maintain control of the motorcycle, and never twist your body while lifting. Check the

motorcycle's controls, footrests, and handlebars for damage prior to riding it again.

The majority of the process of picking up a motorcycle is mental: you need to be smart about it. Even small motorcycles are heavy machines; big bikes are the equivalent of two or even three small

motorcycles. So think about how you want to do it first—if you were going lift a 300-pound refrigerator into the back of your pickup truck, would you just run up and grab it and start muscling it around, or would you plan your attack?

What would you do if it were some double-wide, super-expensive, 800-pound refrigerator?

Step 1: Assess Yourself

Take a few minutes to calm down. Seeing your bike lying on its side can be a traumatic experience, but it happens to everyone at one time or another. Your bike's not going anywhere without you. Spend a few minutes asking yourself questions and talking yourself through it: Are you hurt? Are you able to pick up your motorcycle in a normal situation? Do you want to pick up your motorcycle? Is it safe to pick up your motorcycle? You have the rest of your life to pick up that big bike; take a few minutes to relax and assess the situation. It's best if you get help. And remember: if someone helps you, don't forget to warn them not to touch the hot exhaust pipe, not to lift by the turn signals, etc. Also make sure they lift correctly. You don't want someone else getting hurt.

Step 2: Assess the Environment

If you are in danger from other traffic, get away from your motorcycle and off the road until the overall situation is under control. This may mean letting law enforcement respond and secure the scene before picking up your motorcycle. Take a look at the ground: Do you have a solid surface from which to lift? Is there gravel? Is the pavement wet? Are you right next to a ditch? You don't want to slip and get pinned under your bike.

Step 3: Assess the Motorcycle

Shut the motorcycle off. Turn off the fuel supply if possible. Spilled fuel is common, so use caution (though usually you need sparks, flame, or an ignition source to have a fire or explosion). If the motorcycle is lying on its right side, put the sidestand down and put the motorcycle in gear. If the motorcycle is on its left side, you can't put the sidestand down and can't put the motorcycle in gear. Make a mental note of these facts. You don't want to pick up your motorcycle and then immediately drop it onto its other side!

The Technique

If at all possible, enlist the help of someone nearby!

1. Turn the handlebars to full-lock position with the front of the tire pointed downward. If possible, put the bike in gear so it doesn't try to roll away on you while you lift. If the bike's on its right side, put the sidestand down.

2. Find the "balance point" of the two tires and the engine, engine guard, or footpeg. The motorcycle will be fairly easy to lift until it reaches this point because it's resting on its side. Once you start lifting from there, you are responsible for most of the weight of the bike.

3. "Sit" down with your butt/lower back against the motorcycle seat. Be very careful to keep your back straight and your head up. Put your feet solidly on the ground about 12 inches apart, with your knees bent slightly. With one hand, grasp the handgrip (underhand, preferably), keeping your wrist straight. With your other hand, grip the motorcycle framework (or any solid part of the motorcycle), being careful to avoid the hot exhaust pipe, turn signals, etc.

4. Lift with your legs by taking small steps backward, pressing against the seat with your butt and keeping your back straight. On slippery or gravelly surfaces, this technique probably won't work. On inclined surfaces this can also be very tricky.

Be careful not to go too far . . . and drop the bike over onto the other side!

Superhero style/showoff method. If you've got plenty of muscles and are familiar with wrestling 600-pound bears (and you don't mind beating up the bottom half of your bike a little bit), the bike can be brought back onto its wheels using the "rocking" method. This technique looks pretty cool but is not for the faint of heart and could definitely get you hurt if you screw it up. In general, we don't recommend it. But for those of you who asked, here it is.

1. One foot on the ground, one on the skyward footpeg, front tire pointed down.

2. Rock the bike once, twice, three times to build momentum and get your adrenaline flowing.

3. On the third rock, when the tires touch down, drive one leg into the ground and the other into the footpeg, and wrench that bike into the air.

4. Using this method requires a tremendous amount of power from your legs, arms, and stomach muscles. It's a terrific way for us mere mortals to join the lifetime-back-injury club.

5. Once the center of gravity is aligned more with the tires than the ground, lifting it becomes suddenly much easier.

6. Apologize to the bike for the rough treatment, and expect a little oil smoke on startup (R-type owners only).

Appendix B
Riding Strategy

This book deliberately ignores most of the mental aspects of riding because there are other books with good information in that area: *Ride Hard, Ride Smart, Proficient Motorcycling,* and *Total Control,* to name but a few. But as any rider who's been in the saddle more than a few hours knows, riding is at least 90 percent mental and only about 10 percent physical. What follows is a quick introduction to the art of mental motorcycling that relies mostly on the rider's brain and decision-making skills.

Three Degrees of Separation

On your motorcycle, your riding strategy, physical skills, and protective gear—in that order—are what separate you from the ground. These are the Three Degrees of Separation. By themselves, each of the three degrees can save you. Combined, they create a nearly impenetrable defense against the hazards motorcyclists face every day.

Riding strategy is your first degree of separation because mental skills, as you know, make up 90 percent of everyday riding. One hundred percent attention to your surroundings, accurate detection and perception of road hazards and risks, and sound judgment and decision-making are the primary keys of a good riding strategy.

Attitude also plays a part. Taking responsibility for your own actions is easy, but because you, the motorcyclist, will more likely suffer bodily harm in

the event of a crash, then you, the motorcyclist, must take responsibility for everyone else's actions as well. This means not only being tuned into yourself, your bike, and your environment but also being aware of other drivers, correctly anticipating their behavior, and effectively avoiding hazards before they place you at risk. Ideally, a skilled rider avoids hazards before they even *become* hazards.

Physical skills are your second degree of separation. You acquire them through training, and they require constant practice to keep them sharp. Though they make up only a small percentage of everyday riding, when you really need them, they instantly become 90 percent of your survival. When something breaks through your mental barrier (as any hazard worth its weight is prone to do), instinct, self-preservation, and adrenaline have to take over. At these moments, if your physical response isn't the correct one, you'll immediately need to rely on your third degree of separation: protective gear.

Protective riding gear is your backup in case your first two lines of defense crumble. When something finds its way past your first two barriers, what you're wearing is all you have left. It's technically a combination of the first and second degrees. Mentally, it falls under preparation. Physically, it protects you from the ravages of the pavement and the elements of

heat, wind, rain, and cold that can affect your ability (mentally, again) to concentrate and operate the bike.

In theory, your mental strategy can protect you from everything. For those times when your brain can't save you, your physical skills and ability to control your motorcycle are your backup plan. What your mind and skills can't protect you from, your riding gear has to. Each degree of separation can ultimately stand on its own, but each is far more potent when combined with the others.

Let's look at an example of the three degrees of separation:

Meet Veemax Vince. Vince loves his bike. He uses it for commuting, transportation, traveling, and recreation. He likes the way he looks on his bike. He likes the way it makes him feel.

Unfortunately, Vince doesn't use a riding strategy, has never taken rider training, doesn't ever take the time to practice his skills, and doesn't wear protective gear. He just likes to ride and genuinely thinks he knows how to handle his bike. Anyway, he's ridden for two years without an accident. He knows what he's doing, right?

One day, Vince is on his way home from work. It's 4:30, it's summer, the sun's shining, and the traffic is typical for rush hour. He's wearing penny loafers, slacks, a shirt and tie, and sunglasses. He's riding down Last Chance Avenue, an urban four-laner that has no median, stoplights every four blocks, and a 30-mile-per-hour speed limit. There's no parking on either side of the street, and gas stations, liquor stores, motels, and apartment buildings are spaced evenly apart. Vince is five minutes from work and five minutes from home.

Vince approaches a four-way intersection. He's got the green light, and he's in the right lane. His plan (if you could call it that) is to cruise straight on through at 30 miles per hour. On the far right corner of the intersection is a convenience store. In the right lane, in front of the convenience store, is a big delivery truck, parked illegally, with its flashers on. The truck is blocking Vince's view of the store's exit.

The truck is also blocking the view of Sherry Cavalier, the woman trying to turn left out of the convenience store, behind the truck. She takes a slug of her Coke, sets it down, looks left and right, doesn't see anyone coming, and pulls out—right in front of Vince. Vince's eyes grow as big as saucers, and he panics. He grabs a big handful of front brake and stomps on the rear. Sherry suddenly sees Vince, her eyes grow as big as saucers, and she panics. She slams on her brakes and stops directly in his path.

Vince's ride is over. He slides, both tires locked and smoking, into Sherry's left-front fender at about 20 miles per hour. He is thrown from his bike, and he vaults over Sherry's hood and lands on the blacktop on his head and forearms.

Twenty minutes later, Vince is on his way to the hospital, in a coma, with a fractured skull, broken hand, broken wrist, and snapped collarbone. He's got multiple lacerations on his arms and chest, as well as a heapin' helpin' of road rash. His bike is bent in half and lying in a pool of gas and oil. Sherry, after giving her tearful statement to the police, drives home with a bent front wheel and crushed fender, sipping the Coke she bought forty minutes ago. It's still cold.

Was there something Vince could've done to prevent this? Yes, there was. In fact, there are a number of things he could've done.

First degree of separation: If he'd been using a riding strategy, he would've been more cautious riding through the intersection. He would've known the most dangerous place for a motorcyclist is an intersection. He might have slowed down and been ready with his brakes and clutch to reduce his reaction time. He may have noticed the big blind spot created by the delivery truck and slowed even more or adjusted his position to accommodate it.

Second degree of separation: If Vince had taken rider training, or ever received any instruction or practice in motorcycle skills, he might have known how to use his brakes properly and possibly been able to stop, or at least maybe slow his bike enough to avoid the crash with a quick swerve.

Third degree of separation: Bear in mind that Vince himself never hit the car. He flew through the air and tumbled on hot asphalt. If he'd been wearing a helmet, gloves, and a jacket, he might have gotten up, dusted himself off, and spent the next 10 minutes yelling at Sherry. Then he would've spent the rest of the afternoon mourning the loss of his beautiful bike.

Any one of these three degrees of separation probably would've changed the outcome dramatically in Vince's favor. Had Vince been using all of them simultaneously, this accident likely *never would have happened*.

If you already use the Three Degrees, great. If you don't, it's time to start. If you don't have a riding strategy, create one. If you have never taken a safety course, take one. And if you don't wear protective gear, get some—the best you can afford.

But once you've done all that, is there nothing left? Do you just "stop learning" once you have the Three Degrees mastered? Of course not. Is it okay to be a "pretty good" rider instead of an expert? No way. Is there more to riding than just the Three Degrees? You bet. There's a lot more.

Vince's scenario is based on a true story. It changed the way this author looked at motorcycle riding, and inspired a book on mental riding strategy. The Three Degrees cannot protect you from everything—but they can protect you 99 percent of the time. For ideas on how to protect yourself from the "one percenters," try *Ride Hard, Ride Smart—Ultimate Street Strategies for Advanced Motorcyclists*. In *RHRS*, the Three Degrees of Separation are just a kicking-off point to explore more advanced riding strategies: dealing with other drivers, choosing the safest route, vision and visibility, when not to ride, intersections, risk and hazard hierarchy, speed differential, shadowing, the soft lane change, understanding traffic flow, and group riding, among other concepts. As a bonus, there is an in-depth look at the Hurt Study and what it means today. If you're serious about gaining maximum control of your bike, taking a hard look at your riding habits and developing a strong mental strategy are even more important than the physical skills you develop.

Appendix C

Practice Drill Schedule for Maximum Control

For maximum control of your heavyweight motorcycle, it's not enough to read about the techniques and try the drills a couple of times. Maximum control requires a commitment to ride often, to practice often, and also to practice every time you ride.

This book outlined 10 drills to help you master your big bike in any situation. But having the skills when you need them means they always have to be fresh in your mind. Below is a summary of how often each drill should be practiced.

Riding Drill Number 1	Walk the Line	3 times per week for 20 minutes*
Riding Drill Number 2	Figure Eight	2 times per month for 1 hour
Riding Drill Number 3	Curbside Pullout	1 time per month for 1 hour
Riding Drill Number 4	Iron Cross	2 times per week for 15 minutes
Riding Drill Number 5	Slow and Go	1 time per month for 1 hour
Riding Drill Number 6	Slow, Roll, Look and Press	1 time per month for 1 hour**
Riding Drill Number 7	Inside Line	1 time per month for 1 hour
Riding Drill Number 8	Slow, Swerve, and Go	1 time per month for 1 hour
Riding Drill Number 9	Change Your Line	2 times per season for 1 hour
Riding Drill Number 10	Turn, Brake, Turn	2 times per season for 1 hour

* For Riding Drill Number 1, once you feel you've mastered your friction zone and are able to walk the line in 20 seconds or more, you only need to practice the drill once a month for 20 minutes.

** For Riding Drill Number 6, practice this drill once a month for the first six months of riding or the first six months of riding a bike that is new to you. After that, practice this drill once per riding season.

Presented here is an ideal, generic practice schedule for a six-month riding season. Obviously, these schedules cannot be set in stone, since every rider has a different "second life" (that is, work and family) to attend to in between their riding, but let these schedules be a guide to get you started. Adjust them as you see fit, and put them on your calendar. In time, you'll get used to the routine, and practicing—like riding with complete control—will become second nature to you.

Sample Practice Schedule—Six-Month Riding Season

Month 1	Mon	Tue	Wed	Thu	Fri	Sat	Sun
Week 1	1	4	1	4	1	3, 1*	9
Week 2	1	4	1	4	1	2, 5	
Week 3	1	4	1	4	1	6, 7	
Week 4	1	4	1	4	1	2	8
Month 2	**Mon**	**Tue**	**Wed**	**Thu**	**Fri**	**Sat**	**Sun**
Week 1	1	4	1	4	1	3, 1*	10
Week 2	1	4	1	4	1	2, 5	
Week 3	1	4	1	4	1	6**, 7	
Week 4	1	4	1	4	1	2	8
Month 3	**Mon**	**Tue**	**Wed**	**Thu**	**Fri**	**Sat**	**Sun**
Week 1	1	4	1	4	1	3, 1*	
Week 2	1	4	1	4	1	2, 5	
Week 3	1	4	1	4	1	6**, 7	
Week 4	1	4	1	4	1	2	8
Month 4	**Mon**	**Tue**	**Wed**	**Thu**	**Fri**	**Sat**	**Sun**
Week 1	1	4	1	4	1	3, 1*	9
Week 2	1	4	1	4	1	2, 5	
Week 3	1	4	1	4	1	6**, 7	
Week 4	1	4	1	4	1	2	8
Month 5	**Mon**	**Tue**	**Wed**	**Thu**	**Fri**	**Sat**	**Sun**
Week 1	1	4	1	4	1	3, 1*	10
Week 2	1	4	1	4	1	2, 5	
Week 3	1	4	1	4	1	6**, 7	
Week 4	1	4	1	4	1	2	8
Month 6	**Mon**	**Tue**	**Wed**	**Thu**	**Fri**	**Sat**	**Sun**
Week 1	1	4	1	4	1	3, 1*	
Week 2	1	4	1	4	1	2, 5	
Week 3	1	4	1	4	1	6**, 7	
Week 4	1	4	1	4	1	2	8

This all probably looks like a lot of work. You bet it is. This probably looks like we think you should ride your bike every day. You bet we do. If you want maximum control of your big bike, riding should be a lifestyle and not something you just do for fun once or twice a month with your buddies.

It may not make complete sense just now, but once you're there, you'll know. As the old saying goes, "If I have to explain, you wouldn't understand." Same goes here. Give it your best shot, and a year from now, take a look back and see how far you've come. We're betting you won't even recognize yourself.

Index

RIDE HARD, RIDE SMART
ULTIMATE STREET
STRATEGIES FOR
ADVANCED MOTORCYCLISTS
ISBN 978-0-7603-1760-0

101 SPORTBIKE
PERFORMANCE
PROJECTS
ISBN 978-0-7603-1331-2

101 HARLEY-
DAVIDSON TWIN-CAM
PERFORMANCE PROJECTS
ISBN 978-0-7603-1639-9

MOTORCYCLE
ELECTRICAL SYSTEMS
TROUBLESHOOTING AND
REPAIR
ISBN 978-0-7603-2716-6

TOTAL CONTROL
HIGH PERFORMANCE STREET
RIDING TECHNIQUES
ISBN 978-0-7603-1403-6

HOW TO RIDE A
MOTORCYCLE
A RIDER'S GUIDE TO
STRATEGY, SAFETY AND
SKILL DEVELOPMENT
ISBN 978-0-7603-2114-0

THE HARLEY-DAVIDSON
MOTOR CO. ARCHIVE
COLLECTION
ISBN 978-0-7603-3184-2

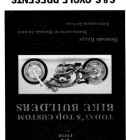

S&S CYCLE PRESENTS
TODAY'S TOP CUSTOM
BIKE BUILDERS
ISBN 978-0-7603-3603-8

THE ART OF BMW
85 YEARS OF
MOTORCYCLING EXCELLENCE
ISBN 978-0-7603-3315-0

Find us on the internet at **www.Motorbooks.com**